SEX
DETOX

Also by Ian Kerner, Ph.D.

Be Honest—You're Not That Into Him Either

She Comes First

Passionista

DSI: Date Scene Investigation

SEX
DET♥X

RECHARGE DESIRE. REVITALIZE INTIMACY.
REJUVENATE YOUR LOVE LIFE.

IAN KERNER, Ph.D.

Collins
An imprint of HarperCollinsPublishers

SEX DETOX. Copyright © 2008 by Kerner-Rubisch, Inc. All rights reserved. Printed in the United States of America. No part of this book may be used or reproduced in any manner whatsoever without written permission except in the case of brief quotations embodied in critical articles and reviews. For information, address HarperCollins Publishers, 10 East 53rd Street, New York, NY 10022.

HarperCollins books may be purchased for educational, business, or sales promotional use. For information please write: Special Markets Department, HarperCollins Publishers, 10 East 53rd Street, New York, NY 10022.

FIRST EDITION

Designed by Kris Tobiassen

Library of Congress Cataloging-in-Publication Data

Kerner, Ian.
    Sex detox : recharge desire. revitalize intimacy. rejuvenate your love life. / Ian Kerner.
    p. cm.
    ISBN: 978-0-06-113607-8
    1. Sex instruction. 2. Sexual abstinence. 3. Couples—Sexual behavior. 4. Single people—Sexual behavior. 5. Man-woman relationships. I. Title.

HQ31.K5143 2008
613.9—dc22

2007028233

For my son Beckett,
conceived in the hungers of love.

"Into love and out again, thus I went, and thus I go."

—DOROTHY PARKER

Contents

Part III: The Singles' Detox

Food for Thought

American sex lives are broken, "shattered," as the old Rolling Stones' song goes—and we cannot seem to make them whole. Our Humpty Dumpty sex lives have left us fragile and fearful. We have lost too many pieces along the way to gather ourselves up, because deep down we believe we're doomed to stumble all over again. While our cultural exposure to sex has heightened over the last decade, our level of personal satisfaction has plummeted to a staggering low, with sexual dissatisfaction being cited more often than ever as a primary cause of divorce. Infidelity is likewise rampant, with women now cheating as frequently as, if not more often than, men. When we find we're not getting what we need at home, we hastily seek it out elsewhere. We are a sex-starved nation, unsure how to feed ourselves healthfully.

Singles are suffering from booty-call burnout, bed-hopping from one fling to the next, desperately searching for something more, without knowing how, when, or where to find it. We treat sex lightly, but sex rarely treats us lightly in return. Younger and younger men are turning to erectile stimulants such as Viagra, while our predilection for anti-depressants continues to wreak havoc on what is left of our libidos. Meanwhile stress, obesity, and lack of exercise are eroding our sexual fitness, as we sit idly in front of our TVs and computers, gazing at pictures of airbrushed, surgically enhanced strangers having sex instead of doing it ourselves. Without even realizing it, we allow boilerplate images and acts to dictate whether or not we are "sexy" and what and whom we desire, without any regard for the unique spectrum of our actual wants and needs. We are bloated and engorged on a steady diet of sexual junk food, but we are far from fulfilled.

Now, more than ever, we need to turn off the noise and tune in to our authentic sexual selves. We need to reclaim our innate erotic potential and rediscover our ability to live vitally and passionately.

The time is upon us to cleanse, rejuvenate, and rebuild our broken love lives from the inside out: to make ourselves healthy and whole again.

How do we begin?

By taking sex off the table so that we can, once and for all, truly feast on love.

SEX
DET♥X

PART I

Getting Started

1.

Doing Without to Eventually Have It All

A PROGRAM FOR EVERYONE—COUPLES, SINGLES, OR ANYONE ANYWHERE IN BETWEEN

The premise of this book is simple: *When it comes to sex and relationships, sometimes we get in so deep the only way out is to start over again.*

For many of us—whether we're in a relationship or actively dating in the hopes of finding that someone special—our love lives have become a source of toxicity, rather than one of sustenance and renewal.

This program is a powerful way to take action in an area of your life that often lacks a clear point of entry: sex and relationships. Think about it: When you want to get in shape, you sign up for a gym membership; when you want to lose weight, you go on a diet; when you want to get out of credit card debt, you consider consolidation plans. But how do you start consolidating your love life?

If you're in a relationship, I'm going to ask you to take sex off the table for thirty days (and, yes, nights too) and give yourself over to the "thrill of the chaste." This is not to say that you *can't* or won't end up having sex in the days that ensue—after all, accidents happen, and hopefully they are ones with happy endings—but rather I implore you *not* to have the kind of sex that is joyless, soulless, or more of the same; bid farewell to the sex that is bereft of the passion, intimacy, and sense of loving connection that you crave and deserve. And if you're stuck in a rut and thinking to yourself that the *last* thing you need in your life right now is to be having even *less* sex, then consider this program the difference between slowly being starved to death in an environment that leaves you feeling desperate and powerless and actively choosing to undertake a diet that you know will result in your becoming a healthier, stronger person both inside and out.

But also know that you don't have to be in a relationship currently to benefit from this program: If you're one of the tens of millions of single people on the hunt for love, and you're feeling burnt out and bruised by the process, it's time to go on a dating detox—to take a break not only from any casual sex you may be having, but to stop dating altogether for the duration of this program and reset for the relationship-results you seek.

Regardless of whether you're single, coupled, or somewhere in between, you only have one love life, and it's time to live it to the fullest.

THE BIRTH OF AN IDEA: TO LIVE AND THINK IN L.A.

Much of this book was written during what turned out to be one of the most romantic periods of my life: when I was doing a six-month production stint away from my family in Los Angeles. I know that doesn't sound terribly romantic, so perhaps I should explain.

I was filming a television program for the Discovery Health Channel that helped couples in long-term relationships overcome difficult hurdles. During this time, my wife Lisa and son Owen came out from New York to visit for long weekends, which never seemed long enough. In between, Lisa and I had resorted to "drastic measures"—naughty emails, breathy late-night phone calls—reminding me of exactly what I was missing on the sizzling island of Manhattan.

When I returned to New York, Lisa surprised me with a "welcome home" dinner, inviting a number of our closest friends. After we were mellowed on merlot and mingling, I half-jokingly asked one of my wife's oldest friends and her husband if they wanted to participate in my program of *limiting* sex to *boost* libido.

"Are you kidding me?" cracked Thea. "When it comes to not having sex, you could take our picture and put us on the cover of your book." Then they chuckled away their discontent with wine.

I turned to Steve, Thea's husband. "When was the last time you were able to feel close and connected to each other without feeling like there was something missing from your marriage, without being painfully aware of what was lacking?"

"Not since Brian was born. What was that, around three years ago, sweetie?" he replied, to which she nodded with sullen embarrassment.

So I seized the opportunity to explain. "What if you could turn that on its heels? Make *not* having sex sexy? What if instead of pretending you were exhausted or sick or too stuffed from dinner or watching a documentary on whale migration patterns, you could embrace and recharge your sense of intimacy by *not* having sex—you know, transform it into something you were not doing *together*?"

They were intrigued, so naturally I pressed: "What if the two of you became achingly aware of *not* touching each other, of *not* kissing, of *not* making love, to the point that one more moment of not being entangled in each other's arms made you feel like a tight coil ready to spring? What if instead of avoiding sex, you promised to ache in longing, to revel in that first touch, that first kiss, to conjure up that extraordinary sense of self- and mutual discovery you once felt as teenagers, but this time with each other?" (I might have been a little less eloquent than this at the time, but I was certainly as passionate!)

"That's a nice idea," said Steve, "but we all know that's impossible."

And that's when I told them: Not only was it possible, it was theirs for the taking. All it required was a decision—they had to be ready to rebuild their libidos from the inside out with that explosive sense of intellectual curiosity, emotional hunger, and physical longing that was present long before they'd begun to worry about mortgages, nursery schools, and love handles.

A mere few days into the detox program, they were rapt instead of laughing. As they went through the process Steve brimmed with sudden desire for a woman he'd taken for granted for as many years as I'd known him. In a matter of days, his wife Thea had been transformed from that comfortable female friend on the sofa beside him to a mysterious, forbidden temptress, capable of igniting his deepest desires.

What I told Steve and Thea that evening is what I'm going to tell you now: Rather than accept the rote menu of sexuality we've screwed ourselves into, you can have the magical, mysterious sex life you've always dreamed of. But to get there, you'll have to deprive your senses in order to feel the full intensity of your aches and longings. Instead of blocking out the fact that you're not having sex, you're going to focus on exactly how that deprivation impacts you at the most visceral level.

Although I call this program a sex detox, its benefits extend well beyond the bedroom. How you love is ultimately an expression of how well you know and love yourself. You will find that the Detox inspires you to engage hidden parts of yourself, bringing to the forefront all of the issues you have with love, sex, dating, general self-esteem, and conflicts that inhibit your desire and ability for intimacy. If there's emotional scar tissue that surrounds your heart, it will be stripped away, rendering you vulnerable but open to positive change. Emotional toxins will be released, revealing patterns of behavior that are masks for deeper fears that have long been hidden.

WHAT YOU'LL ENCOUNTER IN THIS BOOK

In Part I (which you are reading now) I will introduce you to the basic underpinnings of the detox program. Just as a physical fast, or change in diet, will rapidly alter your metabolism and natural body chemistry, so too will a sex/dating detox impact your neurochemistry, enabling you to reset, rewire, and, ultimately, rejuvenate your love life. Not only will the Detox help you to find peace of mind, it will help you transform that new mindfulness into actions that reverberate throughout every aspect of your life.

Parts II and III are more programmatic. In Part II, we'll get into the nuts and bolts of the Couples' Detox, laying out a course of action for you to follow over a focused thirty-day period that includes assignments and exercises in self-reflection. If you're in a relationship, you will learn to see yourself through your own eyes rather than your partner's. You will come to understand your "sexual history" as not just a series of physical encounters, but rather as connected experiences in which the whole is so much greater than the sum of its parts. If you're single, the Singles' Detox will give you a chance to step off the dating treadmill, catch your breath, and recover your inner strength for the road ahead.

But the detox period is only the beginning. If you've ever undertaken a food fast—or any disciplined diet for that matter—you know that the key is to stick with it and sustain the healthy new patterns so that they become a lasting part of your daily life. In Part III, if you're in a relationship, you'll learn how to touch your partner with a renewed sense of passion and possibility. If you're single, you'll recalibrate your aspirations to connect to potential mates from a place of strength and self-knowledge that will eventually bring long-term compatibility.

Whether you're single or coupled, throughout this book you will find case studies of people who were, in one way or another, leading lives of quiet desperation and used the Detox to take action. For couples, our case studies will cover a gamut of sexual issues: low desire, mismatched libidos, boredom; sexual trauma and common sex problems; relationships weakened by one or both partners retreating into a secret world of infidelity or porn, often tuning out and turning off altogether rather than facing basic incompatibility. For singles, our case studies will include issues such as commitment-phobia, anxiety over rejection, the desire for sex versus the need for intimacy, and the fear of always being alone. If you're dealing with or have dealt with any of these issues, I hope the case studies will help you see that you're not alone.

But what if you're ready to reset your love life and your partner isn't on board? If you're single and undergoing the program, it's clearly not an issue. But what if you're married or in a long-term relationship with someone who wants no part of the Sex Detox? All the more reason to give it a try! You can do it, and you can do it alone. Of course, your partner should support you in your mission for self-improvement just as he or she would with any such regimen. But as we know, that's not always the case—and in fact, that may be part of the reason you're undertaking this program to begin with. I would therefore encourage you to stick to your resolution and make a commitment to yourself to see this through. In my experience it's not uncommon for one partner in a relationship to refuse to participate in the process, but powerful changes nonetheless occur when one person decides to take action on his or her own behalf. And who knows—the evidence of your newfound confidence and contentment may well convince your partner to run the gauntlet him or herself after the fact! Either way, the important thing to know is that you will be happier and healthier for it over the long haul.

This what Marilyn, a forty-one-year-old nurse, had to say about the Detox:

"I guess I lost interest in sex mainly because of the kind of sex I was having: boring and routine. I had come to accept that it was just part of being in a long-term relationship. What I found during the Detox is that choosing not to have sex is very different than simply not having it out of boredom or disinterest. In making the choice to go through the Detox, it was my way of saying that I wanted sex to be vital again. I wanted it to be more than just a routine physical act performed out of obligation.

"My husband never did get with the program, so to speak; at least not completely. But I have grown more comfortable with myself, as well as with communicating my needs and desires, and as a result, he's become more responsive and open to change and our sex life has gotten better. I've even begun to take the lead in bed, and I'm shocked at how sexy and strong that makes me feel."

To all of you reading this book, let me offer some advance clarification. Some sections of Part I may not appear to relate to your situation exactly, given that I address both singles and couples. While I have made every effort to be clear about who I am writing for, if you're single and come across the term "sex detox," please think of it more broadly as a period of recharging that applies to *both sex and dating,* and if you're in a relationship and come across the term "dating detox," consider it potentially applicable to your program of *sexual fasting.* You will find Parts II and III (the actual detox and rejuvenation programs) are clearly broken out for couples and singles. Regardless of your relationship state, I hope you will read Part I in its entirety, as it provides an important overview of the program's fundamental principles and may impact you in unexpected ways.

2.

The Science
of the Detox

MORE BANG FOR THE BUCK

We live in a culture of instant gratification and high-speed delights. We don't like to wait, whether it's for a cup of coffee or our one true soul mate. But when it comes to love and sex, a funny thing happens: A delay in gratification makes us want it all the more—and, when we finally do get it, we *enjoy* it all the more.

Writing about the psychology of delayed rewards in his book *Stumbling on Happiness*, Harvard psychologist Daniel Gilbert writes,

> Indeed, thinking about the future can be so pleasurable that sometimes we'd rather think about it than get there. In one study, volunteers were told that they had won a free dinner at a fabulous French restaurant and were then asked when they would like to eat it. Now? Tonight? Tomorrow? Although the delights of the meal were obvious and tempting, most of the volunteers chose to put their restaurant visit off a bit, generally until the following week. Why the self-imposed delay? Because by waiting a week, these people not only got to spend several hours slurping

oysters and sipping Chateau Cheval Blanc 47, but they also got to look forward to all that slurping and sipping for a full seven days beforehand. Forestalling pleasure is an inventive technique for getting double the juice from half the fruit.*

And getting more juice out of your love life is probably one of the main reasons you're undergoing this program.

BRAIN CHEMISTRY AND THE DETOX: A BRIEF SUMMARY

Many of the passages in this chapter contain references to certain neuro-chemicals. These "brain chemicals" affect your love and sex lives in very dramatic ways. And while you don't need a degree in biology to take advantage of the Detox, it is helpful for you to understand the processes that underlie what you're experiencing. For this reason I have included the following overview of the key terms and functions that I refer to in the book.

DOPAMINE: Dopamine is a powerful neurotransmitter that functions as a natural amphetamine. In other words, it gets us focused, excited, and aroused. Dopamine is the reward chemical of the brain, and it plays a key role in both desire and pleasure. The more we pursue a goal, the more our dopamine levels spike, making us want it all the more. Discussing the science behind this delay-reward mechanism as it applies to love, anthropologist Helen Fisher writes in her book *Why We Love*, "When a reward is delayed, dopamine-producing cells in the brain increase their work, pumping out more natural stimulant to energize the brain, focus attention, and drive the pursuer to strive even harder to acquire a reward." As we will discuss later in this chapter, dopamine activity is part of the brain's reward-seeking network. When you think of "the thrill of the chase," it's dopamine that provides a big part of that thrill.

---

* Daniel Gilbert, *Stumbling on Happiness* (New York: Knopf, 2006), p. 18.

NOREPINEPHRINE: Norepinephrine is dopamine's sidekick, riding shotgun along with it. As a stress hormone, norepinephrine controls our fight-or-flight response, activating our nervous system to increase our heart rate and respiration and increase muscle readiness. In terms of love and sex, norepinephrine works with dopamine to keep us focused and on our toes. On the more "toxic" side, it can also keep us hung up on a past love interest.

SEROTONIN: Serotonin is the reason you feel the calm before, during, and after the storm. Serotonin makes us feel calm and balanced, so much so that many of us take selective serotonin reuptake inhibitors (SSRIs) like Zoloft, Prozac, and Paxil to diminish anxiety and keep us calm and collected. When serotonin levels are high, we're cool as cucumbers. Dopamine and norepinephrine are serotonin inhibitors, making us anything but cool and calm when we're in love.

BRAIN CHEMISTRY IN ACTION: HOW THE SEX DETOX WORKS

Couples

When we're in a long-term relationship, sex often loses its newness and novelty and ceases to function as a powerful reward. The natural high of infatuation wears off, and dopamine/noripephrine levels lower. Because we have come to know what to expect, we no longer have that exciting sense of the undiscovered. As many of you have found to your dismay, that hot and sexy partner who you couldn't get enough of becomes just a mate next to you in bed, snoring too loudly and hogging all the covers. For couples, the Sex Detox will show you how to increase anticipation as well as how to re-introduce newness and novelty, naturally raising dopamine levels and helping you to get excited all over again.

Singles

If you're single, please know that you don't have to be in a relationship to benefit from the cleansing effects of a detox; in fact, quite the contrary. Whereas in the Couples' Detox the goal is to "heat up" one's brain chemistry, so to speak, in the Singles' Detox our goal is the opposite: to cool it down.

Whenever I talk to single folks, more than anything else they talk about the stress of dating. From meeting up to hooking up to decoding the abysmal aftermath *(Will he call me? Should I go out with her again?)*, the entire enterprise is riddled with anxiety, insecurity, and uncertainty, and is generally more a source of stress than pleasure. If you've found yourself depressed from the ups and downs of dating, rest assured you are not alone. What you're feeling is, in some ways, part of how our brains are wired.

Stress and anxiety trigger the production of dopamine and norepinephrine (the body's natural amphetamines) while at the same time suppressing serotonin activity (the body's natural mood stabilizer). In short, this neurotransmitter activity puts one on the emotional seesaw that so many daters experience. Dopamine activity is also extremely addictive, so if you're riding the mating merry-go-round it's all too easy get dependent on patterns of behavior.

Writer Rachel Yoder wrote of her personal experience with this in a June 2006 *New York Times* "Modern Love" column: "I had ended a relationship and aware of my tendency to numb my heartache with a new heartthrob, I put myself on a no-dating plan . . . but in a moment of weakness I completed and posted an online dating profile, and soon my inbox was filled with email messages from men, each one a little hit for my addiction. But the high wasn't as fulfilling as it used to be, or maybe I was just too aware of the potential consequences. So I deleted the profile and put my no-dating plan back on indefinitely."

If you're single, undertaking a dating detox will help to naturally lower dopamine levels, increase serotonin, and achieve a sense of calm and centeredness.

Couples and Singles: Same Chemistry, Different Context

Ultimately, whether you're single or in a long-term coupled relationship, you're still human. Single people will, eventually, be part of a coupled romance (that's the point of this, after all!). And coupled people are still individuals. What is different is the context, not the chemicals. For the sake of clarity and ease, the program divides and distinguishes between "singles" and "couples," but when it comes down to it, we're all just people, trying to live our love lives to the fullest.

3.

The Psychology of the Detox

Our own free will may be the strongest force directing the development of our brains, and therefore our lives. . . . The adult brain is both plastic and resilient, and always eager to learn. Experiences, thoughts, actions and emotions actually change the structure of our brains. By viewing the brain as a muscle that can be weakened or strengthened, we can exercise our ability to determine who we become. Indeed once we understand how the brain develops, we can train our brains for health, vibrancy and longevity.

—DR. JOHN J. RATEY,
A USER'S GUIDE TO THE BRAIN

UNLEARNING THE BAD HABITS AND REWIRING YOUR BRAIN

Although I work primarily as a sex therapist, counseling folks on their sex and love lives, I have always been fascinated by the concept of "neuroplasticity," the brain's natural ability to effectively "rewire" itself. While neuroplasticity has long been viewed as a process that characterizes the developing mind during formative childhood years, there has been a good deal of recent debate as to how much of the brain's plasticity survives into adulthood. Can an old dog be taught new tricks? Can we replace old, well-worn neural pathways with new ones?

More and more neuroscientists on the vanguard of brain research are saying yes. And that's good news for us, since much of the Detox is rooted in shifting our thoughts and behaviors. According to Dr. John Ratey, "The brain is not a computer that simply executes genetically predetermined programs. Nor is it a passive gray cabbage, victim to the environmental influences that bear upon it. Genes and environment interact to continually change the brain, from the time we are conceived until the moment we die. And we, the owners—to the extent that our genes allow it—can actively shape the way our brains develop throughout the course of our lives."

What this means for you is that old dating, sex, and relationship patterns can, realistically, be undone—although it wasn't until I had an odd but enlightening encounter with a single woman that I realized why this is the case.

SINGLE AND BREATHLESS

I had just given a lecture at a singles workshop in New York City when a young woman approached me. She seemed despondent, almost lost. She was attractive, thoughtful, articulate, and warm—the kind of woman you'd never expect to have "major issues," at least from external appearances.

"I need help," she confessed after a few seconds of small talk. "I'm suffering from OCD."

I stopped her to tell her that I probably couldn't help her. As a sex therapist and *not* a psychiatrist, obsessive compulsive disorder (OCD) was not an area within my professional expertise.

"No, no. Not *that* OCD," she interjected. "I mean that I suffer from obsessive compulsive dating."

I paused to let that sink in, then smiled and let her continue. *Now* she was speaking my language.

"I'm not in control of my dating life anymore," she said. "I just keep dating and dating like some sort of Energizer Bunny and I can't even tell the men I go out with apart anymore—the dates are just running into one another. It's all a big blur, and I feel like I can't catch my breath. From the incessant checking of my email to the dates themselves to feeling depressed and rejected if I don't hear back from a guy I didn't even like in the first place, I feel like I'm out of control. I lay awake all night feeling like I'll always be alone, that I'll never meet the right guy, that I'll never go on another good date, and that I'll never find 'the one.' I can't seem to turn the thoughts off. And then it all starts all over again."

I talked to her about the benefits of a dating detox, specifically addressing how dating can cause neuro-chemical imbalances (as we discussed in the last chapter). But later that evening I found myself going over our conversation and thinking about her self-diagnosed obsessive compulsive dating disorder and its loose parallels with the real OCD.

Obsessive compulsive disorder is a serious condition marked by a constant barrage of intrusive thoughts and powerful urges that lead to unhealthy patterns of behavior (such as the need to wash one's hands fifty times a day). Those afflicted with OCD often recognize that these intrusive thoughts don't really make sense at a rational level, but they still feel compelled to respond to them. On a biological level, OCD has its roots in brain processes that can be traced to the development of unhealthy neural pathways and consequent chemical imbalances. Treatment often requires a combination of pharmaceutical intervention and rigorous behavioral therapy.

Obsessive compulsive dating was not, in clinical terms, a serious "disease." But wasn't this young woman experiencing irrational obsessive thoughts—that she would never meet somebody, that she was destined to be alone—and then responding to them by compulsively filling her calendar with an endless stream of counterproductive behaviors (in the form of unwanted dates)? And while it might be a stretch to say that this particular form of OCD was rooted in a chemical imbalance, wasn't it possible that hardwired neural pathways reinforced those negative habits and behaviors? If so, was it possible, to a certain extent, to treat dating and love life disorders the same way one treated obsessive compulsive disorder?

DEVELOPING THE ART OF MINDFULNESS

My curiosity led me to the work of Dr. Jeffrey Schwartz—namely his provocative book (with Sharon Begley) *The Mind and the Brain: Neuroplasticity and the Power of Mental Force.* Dr. Schwartz has dedicated much of his life to developing radical, unconventional therapies for the treatment of OCD, based on the expression and exertion of willpower. According to his four-step approach, patients *"Relabel* their obsessions and compulsions as false signals, symptoms of a disease. They *Reattribute* those thoughts and urges to pathological brain circuitry. They *Refocus,* turning their attention away from the pathological thoughts and urges onto a constructive behavior. And finally, they *Revalue* the OCD obsessions and compulsions, realizing that they have no intrinsic value, and no inherent power."

Schwartz correctly reasoned that if patients could learn to reassess their obsessive compulsions and react differently to them through this approach, they would eventually alter the neural pathways that underlie them.

FROM DISORDER TO REORDER

My Detox and Rejuvenation program does not attempt to reproduce Dr. Schwartz's methodology, but it did help me crystallize my thinking. In the pages to come, I will introduce you to a five-step process known as **reORDERing** in which you will *Observe, Recognize, De-Couple, Engage,* and *Regulate.*

But first, a story to ground the process:

Thomas and Mark

Thomas and Mark met at a company softball game. Thomas (thirty-five) was ten years older than Mark, but that wasn't where their differences ended. Thomas had been openly gay since high school, and, having grown up in New York City, had found wide-scale support and understanding among family and friends. He had only rarely experienced direct homophobia. Thomas had sowed his wild oats, and he was ready to settle down in a committed relationship by the time he met Mark. He and Mark had intense sexual chemistry, and they fell head over heels in love. Thomas's background, however, couldn't have been more different than that of his new partner.

Mark had been raised in a working-class family in Detroit with strict religious values. Though he had never officially come out to his family, he knew they were tacitly aware of his "lifestyle" and simply chose to ignore it. In one of his first experiences going to a gay bar in Boston, Mark was threatened by a group of local townies. All of these factors led him to be far less comfortable in his own skin than Thomas, and he therefore preferred to keep displays of public affection to a bare minimum. In Mark's own words, he "wasn't going to pretend he wasn't gay, but neither was he going to go out of his way to let people know."

But none of these differences prevented Mark and Thomas from falling into an intense relationship. The real problems began after they moved in together a year later. That's when Mark lost interest in sex with Thomas—and simultaneously began cheating. Devastated, Thomas kicked him out, and Mark found himself disconsolate, begging for another chance. With great passion and enthusiasm they decided to give it another go, only to find that the same pattern repeated itself. Mark began to lose interest in sex with Thomas, and at the same time found his eyes and hands wandering. But this time, instead of breaking up, they sought counseling.

Since sex was the main way in which their issues were presenting, I asked them to undertake the Sex Detox as we worked together. During the process, Mark pointed to the boredom of domesticity and the ten-year age gap between him and Thomas as the cause of their problem. According to Mark, Thomas was all grown up, ready to be domestic and play house, whereas Mark still wanted to have fun. The term "playing house" came up often enough in my conversations with Mark that I quickly realized there was something more potent brewing beneath the surface.

What soon became evident was that as someone whose sexuality had never been openly accepted by his parents, Mark felt he and Thomas were just "playing" house rather than creating a legitimate life together. This "phoniness"—a word Mark also used often—came to the forefront when he was living with Thomas and, as he put it, "pretending to be married." Unless Mark worked through the issues, he would never experience a sense of authenticity in his relationship with Thomas.

What was important to me was not that Mark confront his parents with the goal of gaining their approval, but rather that he understand how his background was affecting his ability to commit to Thomas fully. During the Detox, Mark was able to start the process of **reORDERing**, which has five stages:

1. **OBSERVATION:** In this early stage of the Detox, we'll use sex and/or dating as a window into fleshing out, and filling in, our personal stories, from our relationships with our parents to the broader cultural and societal influences of friends, family, and the world in which we live. This first step enables us to think about what patterns of behavior we have instinctively and systematically repeated and the underlying experiences that have sustained them. For Mark, the process of observation began by simply allowing himself to recall memories of childhood and adolescence that had been too painful for him to bring to the surface. As an example, once Mark's father realized his son was gay, he stopped hugging Mark, or only did so in a manner that was more awkward than not doing it at all. But seeing his father's warm displays of affection with his brothers led to anger and resentment, mainly at himself.

2. **RECOGNITION:** In this step, we begin to recognize connections between what is happening in our intimate lives with what is happening in the larger context of our lives in general. We will build on the process of observation in step 1 and start to disentangle past from present. In the case of Mark, it meant honing in on key messages and experiences that extended from his parents' views and impaired his ability to take his relationship with Thomas seriously. This ability to identify and explore the basis of emotional reactions within the context of many layers of personal history lies at the heart of neural reORDERing.

3. **DE-COUPLING:** I mean this both figuratively and literally. We need to de-couple our fears and anxieties from their psychological underpinnings and also de-*couple* them literally from others, whether a spouse, casual or serious boyfriend, past lover, or future date. It was important for Mark to stop blaming other factors, such as the

age difference, on his ability to commit to Thomas, and instead to take responsibility for his own actions. By being more connected and aware of his feelings—and the experiences that informed them—Mark was better able to manage his connection with Thomas.

4. **ENGAGEMENT:** Once you've de-coupled, it's time to engage with the world and pursue healthier ways of feeding your actual hunger. This is an ongoing process, and one we will discuss throughout the program. It involves using newfound self-awareness in a positive way, while recognizing the triggers for unhealthy behaviors. In understanding the issues underlying his negative behavior, Mark was able to have more honest and constructive dialogues with Thomas regarding his emotional and sexual needs. It is imperative during this phase of the Detox that we try to mainly engage in behavior that is safe, comforting, and constructive, avoiding anything that might trigger old behavior patterns. When someone flies into a rage at the drop of a hat, or grows intensely insecure or irrationally jealous, possessive, or paranoid, this suggests to me that they are in the grip of "neurally reinforced" habits that have been hard-wired into the brain's "emotion regulation" system. Learning to identify the triggers and stop the negative behavior before it happens, as well as to change automatic responses, is what this Detox is all about.

5. **REGULATING:** This last stage is the ongoing process of *mindfully* managing emotional hunger pangs and cravings without mindlessly succumbing to them. Mark learned to regulate his anxieties going forward so that he didn't revert to his old cheating ways. By learning how to better communicate, understanding his triggers, and giving himself breathing room in the relationship, Mark was able to create an environment that was conducive to and healthy for his relationship with Thomas.

Now, what I've just laid out may sound simple. But rest assured, it takes work and commitment. I have seen scores of individuals and couples struggle, and often fail, to meet their own good intentions. The Oxford dictionary defines "to fast" as "to keep, bind, observe, pledge." During the Detox, the process of reORDERing will help you keep the observations and insights you make, and bind them to positive actions. It is a pledge you make first and foremost to yourself.

4.

Learning How to Read Your Love Map

When most of us think of our "sexual histories," we think about whom we've been with, not who we are or who we want to be. But one of the main goals of the Detox is to gain a better understanding of your sexual history in the *true* sense of the phrase—not in terms of a chronology of partners, but in terms of the key experiences that have shaped your attitudes and inhibitions and colored the landscape of your desires.

During the Detox, you will explore your appetites and discover your own unique sexual fingerprint. This "love map," a term first coined in 1980 by Dr. John Money of Johns Hopkins University, refers to "the sexual template expressed in every individual's erotic fantasies and practices." In other words, our "love maps" represent the blueprint of our erotic desires, shaped by previous positive and negative sexual experiences and explaining everything from why we gravitate to a particular physical type to what feeds our private fantasies and actual practices. Your love map, *not* the number of notches on your belt, tells the real story of your sexual history.

But if there's anything my clinical experience has shown me, it's the daunting number of people who are out of touch with themselves, who have never taken the time to explore their love maps at all. As Plato wrote, "If a person isn't aware of a lack, he cannot desire the thing which he isn't aware of lacking."

How can we go through life unaware of what we lack? At a basic level, we come to sex like we come to food. As children, we are spoon-fed the tastes and habits of those around us, passively coddling our lifelong addictions to (and struggles against) ice cream sundaes, Hershey's Kisses, and McDonald's french fries. By the time we become adolescents, we have similarly been fed an all-you-can-eat buffet of what it means to be sexy and sexual.

As we grow older and wiser, of course, we eventually learn to separate fantasy from reality. But for all our mental capabilities, we cannot completely rid ourselves of our socially constructed cravings. We walk down the street and we see billboards full of people we have been trained to believe are more attractive than ourselves and our partners. We are bombarded with "sexual noise" at every turn. Still, unless we run off to a mountaintop in Tibet, such imagery is inescapable. Or is it?

During the Sex Detox, we will turn off the noise; we will return to our core desires in a more informed way, selectively deciding what turns us on and letting go of those things that don't work for us. Instead of relying on "artificial sweeteners" and "additives," we can explore and determine precisely what kind of longer-term nutritional plan our minds, bodies, and spirits crave, and ultimately make healthier choices that leave us feeling balanced and satisfied.

Let's get going.

PART II

The Couples' Detox

5.

Couples Preparing for the Detox

Over the next thirty days of your life you will be immersed in what I hope is a life-altering experience: the detox phase of this program. If you follow this step-by-step plan (broken up into six five-day modules) and commit yourself to both the Detox and the Rejuvenation phase that follows, you will drastically improve your self-awareness, sexual confidence, and, ultimately, your erotic and emotional lives.

Please note that this is not a miracle plan or a magic act. What you reap will depend on how focused you are and how much effort you put into both thinking about and applying the principles learned here.

As you begin the program you may find that some areas of your sex and/or romantic life are more toxic than others. Some areas may, indeed, be quite healthy. Our goal over the next thirty days is to swing the pendulum from toxicity to health in *all* areas of your love life.

During the Detox, we will cover a lot of ground including your past and present relationships, your sexual development, and your overall sexual health, amongst others. In addition to the Detox Diagnostic with which we'll launch the process, each module contains *Detox Diary assignments* (these typically call for self-reflection) as well as *engagement exercises* that will help crystallize the work you're doing. But remember, the detox period is less about taking overt action—that will come next, during the rejuvenation phase—and more about paving the way for future change by providing a framework for you to do the important work of self-exploration.

In terms of the overall duration of the Detox, thirty days is not an arbitrary number. A month turns out to be just about the perfect amount of time to work through the modules, to rise above the issues, and to purge much of the emotional toxicity. That said, you should feel comfortable working at your own pace. If you finish a module in less than five days, feel free to move forward. But don't rush through them, either. It's not about getting from the beginning to the end as quickly as possible, but giving yourself the chance to let each day's activity make an impact. On the other hand, if you find yourself needing more time, then by all means take it. If you can work through the modules only on weekends, so be it. Better to start the process and proceed incrementally than to not start at all. But, as much as possible, try to undertake the detox sequence continuously, without interruption, in order to maintain a steady sense of deepening self-reflection.

If you're doing this program with a partner, you will find that some of the engagement exercises will ask you to interact with him or her, but that's the exception rather than the rule. Instead, most of the exercises are intended to reinforce your sense of self and individuality—and that means protecting the mental space you're creating during this period of time. In the Rejuvenation stage of the program, you'll have lots of time to engage with your partner and negotiate differences, so take advantage of this time to create a private mental and physical space. Most of us have devoted far too much of our emotional and sexual energy reacting to someone else's wants and needs. The detox period is *your time*—so make sure it's free from partner interference, however well-intentioned. Perhaps you're reluctant to even let your partner know you're undertaking this program for fear of interference or disapproval. It's your time—protect it and make the most of it.

One thing that is very important for you to keep in mind is that, whether you are undertaking this program with or without your partner, you are not going into it alone. Visit www.IanKerner.com, where the *Sex Detox* experience continues.

The Couples' Detox

MODULE 1: STARTING UP
Days 1 to 5

Day 1

PREPARE

Find a private moment where you can take up to a half hour to yourself. Trust me, I know it's not easy: For many of you, finding this small window of time may be the most challenging thing I ask. Ideally it will occur during a time of day and in a physical place where you will be uninterrupted. If possible, dedicate a quiet place in your home to the Detox and return to this same place every day at the same time, as this consistency will give you a sense of comfort and routine, and this place may perhaps even become a source of refuge long after the Detox is over. (Don't worry if that quiet place ends up being a bathroom, rooftop, or even a closet—one guy I worked with ended up sitting in the stairwell of his apartment building.)

Whether you're more comfortable with a notebook and pen or your laptop, you should set up a Detox Diary. In it you will record your thoughts, emotions, and observations. Keep your Detox Diary in a shoe-box (or something similar), which you will also use as a place to store or memorialize letters, photos, and other symbolic images or actual me-mentos from your past that signify important events in your emotional and sexual development. This is more than mere journal keeping; this diary will be a living totem of your Detox and a way to visualize the journey.

BREATHE

Each day before you begin the day's exercise, you will spend up to five min-utes relaxing through controlled breathing. Speaking from personal experi-ence, I always used to find the idea of breathing exercises sort of corny until I actually started doing them with some regularity. I still couldn't tell you whether I'm breathing from "my core" or "taking the good in and letting the bad out," but I do know that you can use some focused breathing to calm and center your mind, and to transition from the outside world into this new private interior space of reflection. As you breathe, try to be conscious of the following:

- YOUR THOUGHTS. Try to empty yourself of thoughts and turn off any internal monologues by focusing on the sound and experi-ence of breathing in and out. If you find yourself unable to re-duce your mental clutter completely, do your best to hone in on the recurring messages and themes so you can record them when you're done, as they will serve as a window into your core anxieties.

- YOUR FEELINGS. Focus on any feelings that may accompany this five-minute breathing period. Does the sense of calm and interior reflection incite guilt or panic? Anxiety or restlessness? Arousal or exhaustion? Boredom?

When you have finished with the five-minute breathing exercise, take two or three minutes to record your "breathing thoughts and feelings" in your Detox Diary.

During the course of the Detox, I'd like you to keep a close eye on how your feelings and thoughts are evolving throughout the entirety of this program. As an example, one woman I worked with, Kristine, who often characterized herself as an "unsexy mom," initially had a hard time tuning out the mundane errands she had to do in her daily life, from buying the week's groceries to dropping off and picking up the kids after school. Even though she had created a private space for herself, she couldn't let herself relax: Her breathing emotions were panic, guilt, and urgency, and her thoughts were of "all the stuff I have to do."

At first, Kristine thought these emotions were about all the things she wasn't getting done—in other words, all the errands and chores clogging her thoughts—but over the course of the Detox she began to realize that her panic and guilt were also about doing something that did not involve giving to others, something that was truly for herself. In other words, she discovered that the underlying emotions that were creating her anxiety were more complex than she'd initially thought.

Toward the middle of the detox period, Kristine realized she was following in the footsteps of her mother, who never took more than a minute to herself between raising three kids virtually on her own. Her mother always looked tired and disheveled, and Kristine pasted an old photo of her mom looking this way in her Detox Diary. Kristine was able to realize through the simple process of doing the breathing exercises, and then writing down her thoughts and feelings, that she and her mother shared similar deep-rooted feelings of guilt and ambivalence about taking time for themselves. This sense of guilt constantly prevented Kristine from prioritizing her own personal care, from getting her hair done to grabbing a quick pedicure to even going to see her doctor. For Kristine, this revelation represented a vital breakthrough on why she associated being a mom with being unsexy.

So think about your breathing thoughts and emotions, and take a few minutes to jot down any connections, both the obvious and the far-fetched. This is your time to think, speculate, and ruminate without consequence or fear of repercussion: Like Kristine, dig a little deeper each day for the hidden connections that lie below the surface.

After you've finished your breathing exercises, you're ready to undertake the next step: evaluating the "state of your union" in the Detox Diagnostic.

THE DETOX DIAGNOSTIC

Please take as much time as you need to answer the following questions. If a particular question is not applicable, skip it. If there doesn't seem to be an appropriate answer or if multiple answers fit, then pick the one that most closely represents your feelings, but write the response that would be more appropriate in your Detox Diary. (Don't worry about your responses—the questionnaire is not intended to be a clinical evaluation but rather a catalyst for contemplating the issues and generally getting the ball rolling.)

How Toxic Is Your Sex Life?

1. Having sex with my partner makes me:

   a. Look forward to the next time we'll be intimate again.

   b. Happy that we had the chance to connect.

   c. Relieved that I got it over with for a while.

2. What I miss most about the early days with my partner is the joy of:

   a. Getting to know each other's passions and pleasures as nobody else had before.

   b. Delighting in how it was bringing us closer to a long-term commitment.

   c. Realizing that if I played my cards right, I could pig out on ice cream in sweatpants forever.

3. When I am naked in front of my partner:

   a. I feel sexually empowered, knowing I am turning him or her on.

   b. I am comfortable knowing he or she accepts me, flaws and all.

   c. I run for cover(s), A.S.A.P.

4. When I recall my childhood fantasies about what sex would be like, I am:

   a. Thrilled that it exceeded my expectations.

   b. Surprised at how different it is from what I'd assumed.

   c. Disappointed that it's not even close to what I thought it should be.

5. Masturbation is something I do:

    a. Whenever I'm in the mood.

    b. If I'm not getting enough sexual gratification from my partner.

    c. Never touch the stuff.

6. Sharing a secret sexual fantasy with my partner is:

    a. Something I'd like to do more often.

    b. Something we used to do back when things were still hot.

    c. Something that would make me ashamed and uncomfortable.

7. When we have sex, my partner is aware of whether I achieve orgasm:

    a. One hundred percent of the time.

    b. Most of the time; I don't fake it, but I generally don't let on either way.*

    c. Doesn't know or particularly care.

8. If my partner found out about what I fantasize about, it would:

    a. Turn him or her on.

    b. Strike him or her as shockingly out of character.

    c. Make him or her disgusted.

9. If I am in the mood to have sex, I:

    a. Grab my partner and go for it.

    b. Snuggle up close to my partner and hope he or she picks up on it and makes a move.

    c. Hit the shower, lock the door, and take care of business myself.

10. If I received a $100 gift certificate for an online sex shop made out to me and my partner, I would:

    a. Tell my partner so we could pick out something fun together.

    b. Buy something just for me and keep it a secret.

    c. Throw it away!

---

* For all of you women out there wondering about the guys taking this quiz, and whether or not men fake it too, the answer is: absolutely.

11. If my partner and I have an argument in the morning, it's likely:

    a. We'll be back in the saddle by night time.

    b. We'll be upset at bedtime, but we'll take a hiatus so we don't go to sleep angry.

    c. We'll sleep in separate beds (figuratively or literally)!

12. When I was young and/or unattached, I usually had sex:

    a. For pleasure and the possibility of romance, without worrying if it didn't lead to a serious relationship.

    b. With the specific goal of finding a long-term partner.

    c. When I was lonely.

13. In my previous relationships, after I had sex with a new partner for the first time, I usually felt:

    a. Happy for the experience and eager for a repeat performance.

    b. More concerned about my performance than my satisfaction.

    c. Anxious that I made a huge mistake.

14. When I think of the single life I left behind, I feel:

    a. Grateful for the memories, but happy to be exactly where I am.

    b. Nostalgic for the good old days.

    c. Disappointed that things only went from bad to worse.

15. If a friend tells me he or she is having really great sex with a new partner, I am:

    a. Happy that he or she is getting a taste of the sweet life.

    b. Slightly jealous, but glad he or she has found someone special.

    c. Envious, but confident he or she will eventually wind up bored and sexless too.

16. When I was single, if I went out on a date and the person didn't make a move on me, I assumed they:

    a. Really liked me, and wanted to wait until we knew each other better.

    b. Didn't like to rush into anything, in general.

    c. Weren't attracted to me.

17. Back when I was dating, when I anticipated having sex with someone for the first time, I felt:

a. Pleasure and giddy excitement, assuming it would be really good.

b. A mixture of desire and caution, realizing this would change the nature of the relationship.

c. Dread and resignation.

18. If my previous partners were asked to describe what I was like in bed, they'd probably say something like:

a. Sexy, uninhibited, and eager to please and be pleased.

b. Neither wild nor uptight, but definitely worth the experience.

c. Would have been better off going it alone.

19. If I were to describe my ideal sexual partner, it would be someone who:

a. Tunes into what I want and tells me what he or she wants so we can enjoy each other fully.

b. Understands that sex is only one aspect of a relationship and not necessarily the most important.

c. Doesn't particularly like sex.

20. If I found out that my partner had a condition that would prevent us from engaging in the kinds of sex we've been having up until this point, I would be:

a. Disappointed, but determined to find new ways to pleasure each other.

b. Concerned that it would negatively impact on our ability to feel close and connected.

c. Ecstatic that I was off the hook once and for all.

21. My parents:*

a. Had a loving relationship that included a lot of displays affection.

b. Were primarily friends and not terribly affectionate.

c. Were not loving or friendly to each other.

---

* Please note that when I ask you to think about your parents, I'm referring to the adults who raised you, regardless of whether or not one or both were your birth parents.

22. My parents were:

a. Open to talking about sex, love, and that kind of thing.

b. Not especially open, but did their best to answer my questions, albeit with palpable discomfort that made me embarrassed to bring up the subject.

c. Not open to talking about sex.

23. My parents:

a. Were supportive of my sexuality and my early romantic interests.

b. Took a "don't ask, don't tell" approach.

c. Were absent or outright unsupportive of my sexuality and romantic interests.

24. I was raised in an environment in which sexuality was:

a. Treated as a normal, healthy, and natural development.

b. Quietly accepted but not openly discussed.

c. Shrouded in silence and/or shame.

25. My first exposures to sexuality came from:

a. Discussions with my parents supplemented by information at school from teachers and peers.

b. Sex education at school, supplemented only by what I could pick up from siblings and peers.

c. Wherever I could sniff it out, say dirty movies and magazines and eavesdropping.

FOR EVERY A, give yourself 3 points.

FOR EVERY B, give yourself 2 points.

FOR EVERY C, give yourself 1 point.

Based on your point tallies, think about whether the general conclusions below are accurate:

If you scored 60 points or more, you are probably still hopeful and optimistic and definitely primed for positive change and more sexual intimacy with your partner. Your upbringing is unlikely to impede your ability to have a healthy sex life.

59

If you scored between 48 and 59 points, you may be a little worn for the emotional wear, but you have plenty of energy left to commit to change and positive growth. You'll have to work on overcoming some of the negative patterns in your past that have marred your sexual self-esteem, but you have the underlying desire and ability to make your relationship work. The values you were raised with are likely to present occasional stumbling blocks in openly expressing and discussing your sexual desires and needs.

If you scored under 48 points, it's most likely going to be a bumpy ride toward positive growth with your partner. You've run yourself ragged emotionally and sexually and feel depleted. You are going to have to work on rebuilding your sexual self-esteem and work on developing healthier patterns of behavior. Otherwise, you will likely wither away in a sexual rut until one or both of you calls it quits. Chances are you find it very uncomfortable to discuss sex openly. If you are suffering from any sexual issues, it is probably hard for you to talk about it with your partner. If you're reading this book, however, it means you are positively committed to overcoming the negative influences of your past and therefore have the potential to have a meaningful and rewarding sex life.

See you tomorrow.

Day 2

As with Day 1, begin with the breathing exercise (turn back to page 30 for a reminder). Once again, the main idea is to clear your head of thoughts and listen to your emotions, and to get to a place where you are truly calm.

Today's main activity is going to involve working in your Detox Diary:

• Take a few minutes to look over the Detox Diagnostic that you completed yesterday. Would you answer the same way today? In retrospect, do you believe you were as honest as possible?

• Now jot down the terms listed below in your Detox Diary. Link the relationships between them and write down the first thoughts, feelings, and memories that spring to mind as part of that association between terms. (I will provide you with an example in just a moment.) Don't worry if you don't use/link all the following terms:

Childhood self-esteem/sexuality
First sexual encounter
Orgasm/satisfaction
Best sex you ever had
Worst sex you ever had
Sexual health
Looking/feeling sexy
Current relationship
Previous relationships
Level of desire/sexual function
Sexual traumas (if any)

This is how Denise, a mother of two who has been married for ten years, completed this assignment:

• **MY CURRENT RELATIONSHIP** is connected to **LOOKING/FEELING SEXY**, because I find it humiliating that I always have to initiate sex with my husband, Mitchell.

• **LOOKING/FEELING SEXY** is connected to **MY LEVEL OF DESIRE/SEXUAL FUNCTION**, because I feel undesirable and self-conscious about my body. If I looked better, maybe Mitchell would find me more attractive, and I would enjoy sex more when I had it.

• **LOOKING/FEELING SEXY** is also related to my **CHILDHOOD SELF-ESTEEM/SEXUALITY**, because my mother was perpetually dieting herself and always told me that unless I lost weight (I've battled a weight problem all my life), no man would ever want me.

- **MY CHILDHOOD SELF-ESTEEM/SEXUALITY** is connected to **PREVIOUS RELATIONSHIPS** and **MY CURRENT RELATIONSHIP**, because I never felt desirable enough to assert my needs in a relationship, both sexually and emotionally, and I've tended to settle for whoever has shown interest rather than choose someone based on mutual interests and compatibility.

And there you have it! Once you get going you'll find it's easy to make connections. And that's the point of this exercise: *that our sexuality is more than just a single aspect or issue; it's an interrelated set of experiences and feelings that have forged patterns, both positive and destructive.* Once we start to get a big picture view of the state of our union, we can isolate and undo recurring patterns that are toxic to our emotional well-being and sexual fulfillment.

See you tomorrow.

Day 3

After you've concluded your breathing exercises (as described on page 30), go back to your Detox Diary and read over yesterday's exercise in connecting the terms. Now add more memories, experiences, and emotions to your story. Here's an example of how Denise fleshed out hers (additions are italicized):

- **MY CURRENT RELATIONSHIP** is connected to **LOOKING/FEELING SEXY**, because I find it humiliating that I always have to initiate sex with my husband, Mitchell. *My friends say I should just do my own thing and focus on improving my appearance and try to make him jealous. But even when I have lost a few pounds and made an effort to look sexier, he doesn't seem to notice. I think he's completely lost interest in me as a sexual partner. It's not fair, since he's even more overweight than I am, and his weight doesn't bother me. I'm just so angry with him for abandoning* *me that it makes me overeat even more. Maybe the reason I can't stick to a diet is that I resent him too much to want to make him happy. He never tries to make me happy.*

As you work through this exercise, take the time to fill in your story. Don't worry about the flow or the editing—just write. Try to let your thoughts flow, uncensored—holding back does you no good. As with every aspect of this program, the more honest you are, the better. At the end of the day, I want you to go back and reread what you've written and add anything new that comes to mind. Also feel free to add pictures or letters or other items to your memory box in order to reclaim ownership of your memories and experiences. Later you will return to these and figure out what you want to keep and what you need to let go of. As an example, Denise found a bunch of old photos and love poems that her husband had written during their courtship, which reminded her of how sexy and loved she used to feel. But she also included some recent photos in which her husband seemed pained even to be standing next to her.

See you tomorrow.

Day 4

Begin with your breathing exercises, then take a few moments to review your Detox Diary. Is there anything you'd like to add or change to any of the entries so far? When you read it over, how does it make you feel? Start today's entry by writing down your thoughts and feelings on the work you've done so far.

Now onto a "touchy" subject that you might not be completely comfortable talking about, reading about, or even thinking about for that matter, but which is nonetheless an integral part of your sexuality: masturbation.

Right now some of you are thinking "big deal," while others of you may be thinking, "oh my . . ." Regardless of whether the subject of self-pleasure makes you blush or cringe, whether it leaves you cold or heats you up, remember that no one is judging you, and one of the main points of this book is to get to know the ins and outs of your unique sexual individuality.

Now, try to think back to the first time you masturbated. Do you remember how it made you feel? Guilty? Excited? Ashamed? Confused? Eager to do it again and again? Do you remember what you fantasized about? Take some time to write it down as honestly as possible. Once you have completed this, I want you to write about your most recent masturbation experience and answer the same questions. Do you think about your partner? Is he or she still a source of sexual fantasy, regardless of the reality?

At the end of the day, I want you to reread both back to back. Are there any similarities? Think about what issues you might have brought with you from childhood and what has changed. Are you more comfortable with your sexuality? Less comfortable? Are there some positive things you left behind? Are there some negative things you've let go of, such as guilt?

And speaking of masturbation, thirty days is a long time to go without sexual release, and I don't want to discourage you from gratifying yourself. The point of the Detox is to learn about your sexuality, cleanse yourself of the sexual toxicity that may have accumulated in your relationship with your partner, and re-approach your love life with a renewed sense of vigor and vitality. By all means, indulge yourself in acts of self-pleasure. Just try to do it a way that is authentic, meaningful, and organic to the work you're doing during the Detox: In short, don't just masturbate out of routine, or boredom, or the need to release some stress, and don't use external triggers (such as porn) to incite arousal. Let the triggers come from within (your thoughts and fantasies) and truly make your orgasm your own. Module 5, "Navigating Your Love Map," is dedicated to this very subject.

See you tomorrow.

Day 5

Begin today as usual with your breathing exercises, and record your thoughts and emotions. Are you able to tune out external noise and interior monologues more often? Are you finding it easier to relax?

Take a few moments to review all the entries in your Detox Diary so far. Add any new images or letters or other items from your past or present that you think illuminate key aspects so far, or make a mental note of any items that might come to mind.

Now briefly answer the following questions:

- After the last few days of reflection, what are the main areas in which you feel you need to focus?

- What are the areas where you feel you are doing okay—maybe even better than before?

- Have your views of yourself started to change? If so, how?

- Are you beginning to see more connections between your past and present? Have you started isolating recurring themes?

At the conclusion of every module, it will be time for some module ending, or "ME," time. This is a gift you will give yourself for undertaking the Detox and for reaching the end of a module. This can include anything from getting a massage to taking a walk in the park. The key thing is it has to be done alone. In addition:

- You have to leave the house to do it.

- It has to be something you've never done before on haven't done in a long time; for example a seaweed wrap, a hike, a trip to a museum, or even a bus ride around the park.

- It should be something that gives you time to let your mind wander. Hence, a movie or a play would not work.

- Place a memento relating to your outing in your diary/memory box.

So—treat yourself to some ME time! You've earned it—just don't forget to write in your journal about it.

Once you've done this, congratulations! You have now completed the first module. In many ways, this is the hardest part—getting started. Take a moment to congratulate yourself on the work you've done so far. I hope you've begun to see how multifaceted and interconnected your sexual history is, and how much of what you experience in the present is rooted in feelings and experiences that may have occurred many years or even decades back.

We've just started the journey, so don't worry if you're still feeling unclear or uncertain about the process. Give it some time. Also, as we discussed earlier, this is first and foremost *your* time, and you're under no obligation to share what you've been thinking and feeling with your partner. On the other hand, thirty days is a long time to keep everything inside, and you may be feeling a strong desire to connect. To that end, consider using the last day of each module as an opportunity to check in with your partner and constructively communicate about the work you've been doing during the detox period. But make an effort to keep the conversation positive and mainly focused on what you've been learning about *yourself.* Approach the conversation in the spirit of constructive communication, not confrontation, and know that you may have knowledge (and hence power) that your partner does not. Use it kindly.

See you tomorrow.

MODULE 2: YOUR SEXUAL HEALTH
Days 6 to 9

This module—*Your Sexual Health*—comes early in the detox program because it's important to gain awareness of some of the factors impacting your sex life that you might not normally think about, such as diet, exercise, sleep, and stress. Developing a "clean bill of sexual health" is a vital part of the program.

In his book on male sexual health, *The Hardness Factor*, Dr. Steven Lamm cites a British study in which men who reported having three or more orgasms per week experienced 50 percent fewer heart attacks and strokes as compared with those who had less frequent orgasms. Lamm's book was inspired by the correlations he made in his own practice between the diminished erectile quality of his male patients and conditions such as obesity, high cholesterol, hypertension, depression, sleep disorders, diabetes, and heart disease.

According to Dr. Lamm, "On the surface, it looks as though the principal message of this study is that having sex reduces the incidence of heart attack and stroke and lets you live longer. In fact, just the opposite is true: being healthy allows you to have as much sex as you want."

This statement is equally true of both women and men. Your sexual health and overall health are intimately connected to each other. The goal of this module is to both determine your level of sexual health and get you on the road to improvement in those areas that need it.

Day 6

Today, after your daily breathing exercises, you'll consider a number of categories of sexual health and explore how they apply to you. Each of the categories listed below will pose a series of questions that I'd like you to answer in your Detox Diary. During this time, I'll ask you to think back to health issues or medical problems you might have experienced to determine their relationship to sexual desire and function.

GYM DANDY VS. COUCH CANDY: THE EXERCISE FACTOR

Regular aerobic workouts help to keep the blood flowing and the arteries producing nitric oxide. Nitric oxide is the lifeblood of sexual arousal. Men who don't exercise are much more likely to experience bouts of erectile disorder than those who do, women who don't exercise are also more likely to experience arousal issues. Not only is overall blood flow heightened during aerobic exercise, but feel-good endorphins (natural opiates) that contribute to relaxation and sexual arousal are also released. Exercise also plays a major role in generating positive self-esteem (a subject we'll talk about more later), which is perhaps the most powerful sexual enhancer.

Answer the following questions in your Detox Diary:

• Is exercise a regular part of your lifestyle?

• Think back on various times in your life when you exercised more or less. Do you see any relation to periods of high and low desire?

• When you exercise more, does it make you feel more sexually confident and desirable?

• If you don't have time to get to the gym, what other ways can you make exercise part of your daily routine?

EATING YOUR HEART OUT: THE FOOD FACTOR

A poor diet is a major contributor to heart disease, high cholesterol, arterial plaque, and high blood pressure, among other conditions, all of which inhibit blood flow to the genitals and impact both desire and arousal. So what's key to the "desire diet"? Eat for the heart, and you're eating for desire. Now I'm not about to prescribe a precise food regimen (there are more than enough diet books on the shelf!), but I will tell you that one of the keys to a healthy diet is the idea of nutrient density. In short, when the ratio of nutrients to calories in a food is high—as is the case with most vegetables—fat burns off and health is maximized. Hence, the more nutrient-dense foods you consume, the more you will be satisfied with less calories, and the less you will crave more high-calorie foods.

Answer the following questions in your Detox Diary:

- Do you make an effort to eat nutritionally balanced meals?

- Do you avoid junk food, saturated fats, and foods high in processed sugar, that is, empty calories?

- Do you consider yourself overweight?

- Do your eating habits leave you energized or lethargic?

- Do you turn to food for comfort or as a response to anxiety?

- Do you often snack between meals?

- Are you relatively happy with your body and fitness level?

SEXUAL TENSION: THE STRESS FACTOR

All stressed up with nowhere to go? Stress can take a major toll on your sex life. For men, work-related stress is particularly likely to inhibit desire, while women are often more susceptible to stressors that originate at home. Obviously, our sex lives themselves can be a source of stress and anxiety, all of which can create a vicious, destructive cycle. This program is designed to help you reduce the stress you may be feeling or at least learn how to keep stress from impacting your sexual health.

Answer the following questions in your Detox Diary:

• Do you feel as if you're living with chronic stress?

• Can you remember periods of your life when you weren't feeling stressed? What was different about your life then?

• Can you identify the various sources of stress in your life?

• Have you attempted methods of stress reduction, such as yoga or exercise, or meditation?

• Do you overeat or use chemical assistance (alcohol, cigarettes, pre-scribed or non-prescribed drugs) to abate stress?

• Does stress diminish your sex drive and/or interfere with your ability to remain aroused or focused during sexual interactions?

• Does sexual release help you relax?

Do you argue in a way that's bad for your health? More and more re-search is indicating that it's not what we argue about that matters as much as *how* we argue—our approach to confrontation can exact as big a toll on our health as other factors such as diet and exercise.

Arguing naturally triggers the brain's "fight or flight" response system. Many men respond by fighting, and it's been shown that this confronta-tional approach raises one's heart rate, increases blood pressure, and plays a big role in cardiac disease. But interestingly, the opposite reaction, flight, can be just as harmful, if not worse, to women. It leads to self-silencing: a bottling-up of emotions that causes anxiety, depression, and a cascade of unhealthly behaviors.

Not surprisingly, sex is one of the main reasons people argue, often above money, housework, and other common sources of conflict. Sex is also one of those subjects that women tend to keep bottled up because they're afraid of eliciting an angry reaction. You can be lying in bed next to someone and feel a million miles apart from him. Later, we'll explore specific approaches to arguing more healthfully, but for now think about how you and your partner argue and whether or not you're expressing yourself healthfully.

ONCE UPON A MATTRESS: THE SLEEP FACTOR

Sleep is as vital to our physical well-being as food and water, and even a single restless night will find its expression in higher levels of stress and lower levels of arousal. Conversely, those who are well rested are more able to have better sex.

Answer the following questions in your Detox Diary:

- How much uninterrupted sleep do you get each night on average?

- Do you know how much sleep your body needs to feel well rested and regenerated, keeping in mind that different people have different sleep needs?

- How many nights per week do you suffer from insomnia?

- By the time you go to bed, are you generally too tired for sex?

- Does sex or masturbation help you sleep?

- If your partner is already sleeping, does that make it easier or harder for you to fall asleep?

- Do you take any form of medication or pill to help you sleep? If so, how dependent are you on this source?

- If you're unable to sleep because of racing thoughts, have you tried alternatives such as yoga, deep relaxation techniques, or writing in a journal to help clear your mind of the thoughts that keep you awake?

• Are there any other factors that might be affecting your sleep, such as the adrenal fatigue related to menopause?

ANIMALS, VEGETABLES, AND MINERALS (OH MY!): THE VITAMIN FACTOR

L-arginine, an amino acid, is a building block of protein and converts to nitric oxide, which, as we discussed earlier, is vital to sexual arousal. Pycnogenol is a combination of many antioxidants extracted from the bark of a pine tree and is known to protect the heart, fight those nasty free radicals, and increase sexual arousal. Omega-3s, which are found in certain fish oils, reduce plaque that builds up in arterial walls and impairs blood flow, hence increasing levels of sexual arousal and response. Vitamins C and E are powerful antioxidant supplements that protect against free radicals and reduce fatty deposits in the blood. Most of these vitamins and minerals can be found in a quality multivitamin, or simply by eating nutritiously.

Answer the following questions in your Detox Diary:

• Do you make an effort to eat balanced meals and meet daily recommended nutritional requirements?

• Do you take a multivitamin or other supplements?

• Do you have any symptoms, such as a tendency to easily bruise, bleeding gums, dry hair, or brittle nails, that might indicate a nutritional deficiency?

• Do you notice a difference in the way you feel emotionally, physically, and sexually when you are eating for health rather than simply to maintain a desired weight?

OH, MY ACHING HORMONES: THE AGE FACTOR

As we age, both men and women may find themselves taking longer to become sexually aroused, or even losing interest in sex altogether. In men, waning testosterone levels can make a guy moody, irritable, and depressed.

Decreased testosterone also places men at a greater risk for heart disease, as well as making them more prone to injury due to decreasing bone density. For women, changes in sexuality associated with menopause may affect lubrication, arousal, orgasm, and overall sex drive. But, without a doubt, one of the more pronounced symptoms related to menopause (as well as its early onset during peri-menopause) is reduced libido. But even so the capacity to have satisfying sexual relationships does not disappear with age. We remain sexual throughout our lives, and many couples find that sex becomes more intense and intimate as they age. It's not as simple as "less hormones = less sex." It's all about lifestyle: exercise, diet, sleep, and a healthy engagement with life. By understanding the inevitable changes that occur over the sexual life cycle, and knowing how to deal with them, you can sustain a healthy, satisfying sex life well into your golden years.

Answer the following questions in your Detox Diary:

- Has your sexual response changed with age? Do you find it takes longer for you to get aroused or reach orgasm? Are you less physically responsive?

- Has your level of sexual desire changed with age? Do you find you are less interested in sex in general than when you were younger?

- How do other physical aspects of the aging process, such as reduced physical strength and stamina or visible signs of aging, impact your sexual confidence and interest in sex?

- If you've gone through menopause, have you taken either prescription or holistic supplements to offset the hormonal shifts of aging? How did they impact your sexual function and level of desire and arousal? If you're a man, have you had your testosterone levels checked?

HIGH AND DRY: THE DRUG AND ALCOHOL FACTOR

We all know that tobacco contributes to lung and heart disease, but many people don't realize that it seriously affects sexual health as well. Smoking damages the arteries affecting blood flow to the genitals, and it leads to a loss of desire and arousal in both men and women. In terms of alcohol consumption, most of us know that having a drink or two before sex may help us relax and ease our inhibitions. But high levels of consumption can also result in sexual dysfunction. From causing the loss of erections to preventing your ability to get or stay aroused, alcohol disables the natural sexual response of the autonomic nervous system. Other chemical substances, like marijuana and cocaine, also have known links to low sex drive and sexual dysfunction.

- Do you smoke cigarettes? If so, how frequently, and for how long have you been smoking?

- Have you noticed a corresponding increase or decrease in desire and function when you've abstained or cut down on this habit?

- Does your partner smoke?

- Do you use alcohol or other substances to help you relax or loosen up? Do you rely on it to have sex?

- Has alcohol or other drug use ever impaired your sexual function or contributed to negative sexual experiences?

THE PHYSICAL WELLNESS FACTOR

From temporary ankle sprains to lifelong high blood pressure to seasonal hay fever allergies to insulin-dependent diabetes, many of us suffer from health issues that require immediate to long-term treatment and care. It is important to realize that both the condition(s) and treatment may have some impact on your level of desire and sexual function. Even something as simple as going on the pill can wreak havoc on your libido. But regardless of what particular problems you may be suffering from, you can still find ways to incorporate sexual and emotional intimacy into your life. What is essential, first and foremost, is your willingness to accept yourself and feel sexy and sexual.

- Do you have a temporary, recurring, or long-term medical condition that directly impacts your general sense of well-being? Have you had one in the past?

- Have you found that during acute periods of affliction your sex life has been affected either by the condition itself or by the medication(s) you take for it?

- How much of this impact is caused by negative emotions surrounding the health condition?

- Are you currently taking any medication? If so, are you aware of any possible sexual side effects?

- Have you talked to your doctor about how to manage them, or asked if other alternatives are available?

- Have you talked to your partner and explained how your condition or treatment is making you feel?

See you tomorrow. (Please note that tomorrow's engagement activity commences at the start of the day, so either read through the instructions now, or make sure you can clear some time in the morning to prepare yourself.)

Day 7

The following **engagement activity** is something you will be actively doing throughout the rest of the day. As you go through your day, think about how each daily activity affects your sexual health and whether it fundamentally *helps* you or *hurts* you. Take notes as you go along.

At the end of the day, list each activity in your Detox Diary.

For example, Fernando, a pharmaceutical sales rep in his mid-thirties, came up with the following:

- Skipped breakfast. (HURT)
- Ate McDonald's for lunch. (HURT)
- Cancelled a gym appointment with his trainer. (HURT)
- Stayed late at work to finally finish a deadline that had been stressing him out. (HELPED)
- Prepared a salad with low-fat dressing and steamed fish with vegetables for dinner instead of ordering in pizza. (HELPED)
- Read in bed with his wife and snuggled. (HELPED)
- Resisted the urge to check out a porn site after his wife fell asleep. (HELPED)

Once you've written through your day, take a good look at your list and flesh it out. Are there more "hurts" than "helps"? What else could you do that would help? Are there behaviors that could be altered to move them from the hurt to the help category? What do you think your partner's list would look like?

See you tomorrow.

Day 8

As always, begin by doing your breathing exercises. Today, we will repeat the **engagement activity** we did yesterday—but I want you to try to improve the ratio of "helps" to "hurts." As an example, Janice, a lawyer in her thirties, did the following:

- Walked halfway to work before getting on the subway, and walked all the way home. (HELPED)
- Brought a healthy lunch instead of going to the cafeteria. (HELPED)
- Skipped afternoon cigarette break. (HELPED)

- Grabbed a handful of candy sitting by the copy machine. (HURT)
- Drank too much coffee. (HURT)
- Cancelled a squeezed-in social obligation to make her day less hectic. (HELPED)
- Called her mother to discuss a comment she made that was keeping her up at night. (HELPED)
- Hung up the phone on her mother in anger. (HURT)
- Called her mother back and apologized and told her she was still hurt by what her mother had said. (HELPED)
- Stopped off at a vitamin store and picked up some multivitamins. (HELPED)
- Shut off her computer and went to sleep at a reasonable hour, ignoring work emails that could wait until the next day, and slept for eight blessed hours. (HELPED)

Compare today's list with the one you completed yesterday. Do they look different or similar? Were you able to make improvements with just a little bit of effort, or do you still need to think harder about the activities that help and hurt your sexual health, and how to do more of the former? Don't worry if you weren't able to make dramatic changes, but instead focus on incremental changes that are within your power.

For example, Janice has a number of food intolerances that she often chooses to ignore in the service of being a good sport with her husband—wheat makes her congested, and raw garlic and onion give her intense gastrointestinal distress, but her husband has always loved dishes that use these ingredients. While these intolerances cannot be eliminated, she has the ability to manage them better by avoiding certain types of food.

Now, elaborating on the above, I want you to take a moment to write about your efforts to improve your health, and whether they are negatively affected by your partner's behavior. Also consider whether there is room for compromise. Let me give you some examples from my patients:

Fitness: "I'd like to spend an hour at the gym after the kids go to sleep, but my husband says it cuts into our time together." Compromise: Jump rope at home.

Depression: "My current anti-depressant medication helps my depression, but it makes me less interested in sex and makes it harder for me to reach orgasm." Compromise: Look into alternative treatments and make sex more sensual rather than orgasm centered. Spend more time on foreplay.

Nutrition: "I'd like to go on a primarily vegetarian diet, but my wife says she's a carnivore and proud of it." Compromise: We prepare separate meals side by side and still eat together.

Take a few minutes to write out your own set of potential compromises and think about how your partner would respond to them.

See you tomorrow.

Day 9

MODULE ENDING ("ME") TIME:

It's time for another "ME" time activity. See page 42 for a reminder on the general rules, and be sure to take some time to think about and write about where you are, both in terms of where you started and where you hope to be by the end of this journey. Most of all, congratulate yourself on the progress you've made so far in becoming a healthier, more sexually confident and satisfied person. (Remember, this may be a good time to connect and constructively communicate with your partner about the work you've been doing during the detox.) Try talking about some of the activities and issues in your daily life that hurt or help your sexual health. Focus on the ones that don't involve your partner.

See you tomorrow.

MODULE 3: SEXUAL SOCIALIZATION
Days 10 to 15

In order to create and sustain healthy intimate relationships, we need to go back to the original building blocks of our "sexual socialization" and see how our patterns of sexual behavior took shape. Over the next few days of this module, you will be asked to examine how you were "modeled"—or, in other words, what you learned and internalized about sex and relationships throughout your childhood and adolescence, and how those experiences affected the ways you "mate and relate."

As you work through the activities in this module, you will find that some of the connections between your past and present are clear while others may seem vague and indirect. But because sex is ultimately a very tangible expression of how we love, it's important to pay attention to both the sexual and non-sexual aspects of our development and socialization. By isolating the various threads that make up our socio-sexual tapestry, we can better understand the elements that detract from the big picture of what we want and who we *choose* to be.

Day 10

As always, begin with your breathing exercises. Do you feel calmer, more centered, and able to focus on the simple sensation of breathing?

Now, please answer the following questions in your Detox Diary:

1. From what I know and remember of my earliest years, physical affection was a regular source of comfort and love. *(Do you remember your mother or father tucking you in with a kiss at night? Do you have early memories of being picked up and hugged by one or both parents? More one than the other?)* True or False? Please elaborate.

2. My parents had different approaches to providing affection to my siblings and me. *(For instance, in many cases, fathers are more comfortable rough-housing with boys than girls.)* True or False? Please elaborate.

3. Growing up, my parents were always affectionate with each other. *(Do you remember your parents hugging or kissing? Did they seem physically comfortable and connected? Were they cold and distant?)* True or False? Please elaborate.

4. My parents employed physical means of discipline. *(Did your parents ever reprimand you with a hand or belt? Was the method routine? Was it specific to only one parent? Was physicality something you associated more with punishment than affection in your childhood?)* True or False? Please elaborate.

5. As I grew older, my parents were less comfortable showing affection. *(Were your parents more standoffish as you matured through puberty and adolescence? Were you aware of any differences in how your mother and father physically interacted with you? How did you perceive the difference, if any?)* True or False? Please elaborate.

At the end of the day, reread your answers. Do they stir up any additional memories or images? Take a few deep breaths and decompress.

See you tomorrow.

Day 11

Start with your breathing exercises.

PICTURE THIS

Today we will be looking through as many old photo albums, slides, and home videos as you can get your hands on, specifically looking at images of physical affection in your family. In particular, I'd like you to take notice of any changes in the quality of physical affection as you grew older. Were your parents less physical with you as an adolescent? Were there significant differences between how your mother and father engaged with you and your older and younger siblings? How does it make you feel when you see these images? Do you look happier or sadder than you remember? Do any of the photos seem staged or artificial? If the photos trigger memories of special events or occasions, how did your family interact at those events? Did they seem to act differently when in the presence of other people than during candid moments alone? Take a few select photos out of your album—the ones that give you pause, for better or worse. Place them in your memory box.

As you go through your day today, I'd like you to pay special attention to parents interacting with children. Make an effort to walk by a schoolyard or playground or soccer field. Go to the supermarket or an ice cream parlor or the corner market. What do their interactions look like? How do they compare with the photos you looked at earlier? Do they seem more or less affectionate than you were with your family? Does this stir up any other memories or feelings? As an example, Claire, thirty-two, grew up as an only child with a father who was extremely protective and constantly fretting over her safety. As a result she developed tremendous anxiety, always avoiding any situation that presented any potential risk. Although she had received her driver's license as a teen in the suburbs of New Jersey, it had long since expired, and getting behind the wheel always terrified her. In fulfilling this engagement activity and watching fathers interact with their daughters in the park, she was struck by how free the little girls seemed, and how the fathers supported and encouraged them in activities like climbing the jungle gym, which her father had always deemed too dangerous. It didn't take long for Claire to also connect this sense of anxiety (inculcated by her father during childhood) with later anxieties such as the perpetual fear of pregnancy whenever she was sexually engaged with a male, regardless of his use of a condom. Claire had fully embodied her father's anxiety. How would your partner answer these questions?

Think about your own connections and associations.

See you tomorrow.

Day 12

Today we will begin by looking back at how we related physically to our parents during childhood. Please answer the following questions, circling the answer(s) that best apply below or writing it out in your diary. Feel free to add to the list, and be sure to elaborate if you feel the need!

1. When I was touched by my parent(s) as a child, I generally felt:

  loved   secure   anxious   avoidant   detached

2. When I am touched by my partner, I generally feel:

  loved   secure   anxious   avoidant   detached

3. When I hugged or kissed my parent(s) as a child, I generally felt:

    loved   secure   anxious   avoidant   detached

4. When I cuddle or snuggle with my partner, I generally feel:

    loved   secure   anxious   avoidant   detached

Did you notice any correlations between how you responded to the questions? Take a moment to think about how your experiences as a child affected your experiences as an adult.

For example, Kendra, thirty-six, felt loved by her partner, Shelly, thirty-eight, but sometimes felt as if she had to be strong enough for both of them. From an early age, Kendra knew she was gay, and her mother was incredibly supportive. She was always able to bring girlfriends home, and Kendra's mom never chastised her or tried to dissuade her from dating women. Kendra attributed a large part of her mother's tolerance to having survived a bad marriage and getting much emotional support from female friends, as well as to her mother's experiences as an ardent feminist in the 1970s. Shelly's experience, however, was radically different. At the time recently out of the closet after an unhappy marriage, she was still not out to her immediate family and co-workers. She was uncomfortable hanging out with Kendra's primarily gay friends, and she often wondered whether she was simply going through "a lesbian phase."

Whereas Kendra used touch to express tenderness and desire, and was confident in her sexuality and her ability to love and be loved, for Shelly, touch often triggered anxiety and feelings of detachment. When Kendra touched Shelly, she typically felt Shelly flinch.

In Chapter 4, we discussed replacing negative habits and thoughts with positive ones, and leveraging your brain's natural propensity to re-wire itself through a process known as neuroplasticity. As I discussed, the process I've dubbed **reORDERing** allows you to:

Observe (in this case your childhood),

Recognize patterns and behaviors that might have been modeled without realizing it,

De-couple your learned responses from their present form in your daily life,

Engage in new ways that allow you to self-soothe, and, ultimately, Regulate yourself as you move forward.

For Shelly, reORDERing meant learning not to emotionally vacate or fall into detachment mode when touched. The starting point in the process came in observing her current relationship with Kendra and its connection to both previous relationships as well as her childhood. Shelly felt that her emotionally abusive ex-husband was at the root of her anxiety about being touched, which she explored throughout this Detox.

But Shelly also had a father who was cold and remote. He rarely hugged her and was often icy or quick to shrug her off when approached. Shelly observed that during those times when Kendra hugged her and she felt herself detaching, it was similar to how she felt when her father withdrew from her and that she was modeling the behavior she had grown up with. For Shelly, the reORDERing process began with **Observing** the situation and **Recognizing** that she was responding to Kendra much the way her father had responded to her. But unlike her father, Kendra is an intimate affectionate partner, and so Shelly had to **De-couple** the feeling of detachment from Kendra and realize it was not a function of the relationship. Instead, when she engaged with Kendra, she had to be conscious of her tendency to detach, especially as it was often a trigger for a larger feeling of depression. Touch often compelled her to detach and isolate. Shelly was able to engage in a new pattern of behavior with Kendra by holding an embrace and touching to feel connected until the impulse to detach subsided. Normally when she hugged Kendra she would quickly pull away and break the embrace, but now she consciously focused on hugging through her anxiety and getting to a place where she felt calm and connected. This allowed Shelly to **Engage** more constructively and **Regulate**. Shelly mapped out the process of reORDERing as follows:

- **OBSERVE** an instinct to detach upon being embraced.

- **RECOGNIZE** the same sense of detachment as when she hugged her father and later her husband.

- **DE-COUPLE** the sense of rejection/anxiety of being hugged from her current relationship with Kendra.

- **ENGAGE** with Kendra in a new way, namely hugging "through" connection. (This part took practice.)

- **REGULATE** the instinct to vacate and replace it with a positive mode of behavior.

Look over your own responses from above and pay attention to the negative emotions you circled in connection to being touched both in the past and the present. If and when you identify a connection (a negative behavior that has survived from childhood and is repeated in your current relationship), attempt to map out your own alternative behavioral pattern the way Shelly did. Remember, it takes time to work through your ingrained reactions to time-hardened, neurally reinforced behaviors. So do your best, be patient, and realize that practice may not make perfect, but it will make things better.

At the end of the day, reread all your entries throughout this module. How do they make you feel? Look through all the images you gathered and add any new photos or notes to yourself that highlight a key issue or memory. Then take a few deep breaths and decompress. You can practice **reORDERing** with your partner, if it feels right; if not, there's no pressure. You can visualize it instead for now and think about how it makes you feel. Or, like Shelley, start with something simple and direct like a hug and pay particular attention to both of your responses.

See you tomorrow.

Day 13

Today we are going to spend a bit of time reflecting on gender assumptions, particularly what it means to be "male" or "female" and how your past shaped your sense of yourself as an adult woman or man.

Despite the growing overlap, there still remains a fairly pronounced gender bias in domestic tasks and childrearing. Even though we may have grown up in an age of greater equality between the sexes, many of us still came from homes where our fathers had more demanding careers than our mothers, and our mothers did more of the household chores and family rearing.

To better explore how your gender assumptions were modeled during childhood, please answer the following questions in your Detox Diary:

- Were the female members of your family treated differently than the male members?

- Was there a double standard regarding your parents' responsibilities in tending home, finances, and family? Was this double standard echoed in how you and your siblings were treated?

- Looking at your parent of the same sex, to what extent do you think you've modeled and/or rebelled against the gendered behaviors he or she espoused?

- How do gender roles affect your sexual behavior? Does the male member of the couple generally take the lead in making sexual overtures? Does the female member feel more inclined to dress or look sexy than the male?

- Do you feel you have positive role models of the same sex? Are there negative stereotypes you consciously avoid? For instance, if you're a woman, do you fear being seen as aggressive, and if you're a man, do you attempt not to seem wishy-washy?

- Do you think about your sex life in the context of sexual stereotypes, such as "men always want more sex than women"?

As a means of testing yourself on your sex/gender bias, answer the following true or false questions without pausing to censor yourself:

1. Men typically have more sexual experience than women. True or False?

2. On a date, a guy should make the first move. True or False?

3. Men should always pay on a date. True or False?

4. Men should take the lead sexually. True or False?

5. Men are logical; women are emotional. True or False?

6. If a woman goes to bed with a guy on the first date, she's easy. True or False?

7. A woman should never go on a date within twenty-four hours of being asked. True or False?

8. Once a man gets an erection, a woman has an obligation to give him some form of release. True or False?

9. Men are better at geography and sports. True or False?

10. Men don't get as attached as women. True or False?

11. Women should accept male attention as a form of flattery. True or False?

12. Men usually want to have sex for the sake of conquest. True or False?

13. It's normal for men to stare at women. True or False?

14. In every man there's a little boy. True or False?

15. A woman who has sex before the third date has blown the possibility of a real relationship. True or False?

16. Every woman who is single wants a man. True or False?

17. When a guy gets sexually excited, he loses control. True or False?

18. If a woman sexually excites a man and doesn't deliver, she's a tease. True or False?

19. A woman should be careful about revealing her number (of past sexual partners) to a man. True or False?

20. Women use sex to manipulate men. True or False?

21. In most gay couples, one person is the top and the other the bottom. True or False?

22. Men are more violent and easier to excite than women. True or False?

23. Women stop having sex once they get a ring on their finger. True or False?

24. A man needs a woman to take care of him. True or False?

25. Women who play games and lead men on get better boyfriends. True or False?

26. If a guy pays for a date, he deserves or expects some sexual attention in return. True or False?

27. Men take risks; women play it safe. True or False?

28. Women should always dress sexily to keep their man interested. True or False?

29. Gay men are more sensitive than heterosexual men. True or False?

30. Lesbians are less emotional than straight women. True or False?

32. Men are thrill-seekers; women are not. True or False?

33. If a man is insulted, he needs to stand up for himself. True or False?

34. If a man's girlfriend is insulted, he needs to stand up for her. True or False?

35. If a woman is hanging out at a bar alone, she's looking to hook up. True or False?

36. Women cry to manipulate men. True or False?

37. Sexual prowess is a sign of masculinity. True or False?

Review your answers to the above questions. Are you surprised by any of your responses? How many were met with a gut response of "true"? To what extent do you still subscribe to ingrained gender stereotypes? When there is something to be fixed around the house, is it tacitly assumed that's the guy's job? If there's a dinner party in the making, is it assumed that the woman of the house will take the lead? Who does the nitty-gritty household work like cleaning the toilets and the kitchen? Who is responsible for making social plans? The list goes on and on. Now, make a list of routine domestic activities and chores to see how you and your partner conform to or contrast with traditional gender stereotypes. Take Jean and Carl, both in their forties, for instance. Married with two kids, Carl does most of the cooking and childrearing (contrast), but Jean still does most of the cleaning and household chores (conform). Carl is responsible for making social plans (contrast) and Jean is usually the one to initiate sex (contrast). How do you stack up? Are you surprised? Annoyed? Keep in mind that there is nothing inherently better about conforming vs. contrasting, although frequently "contrasts" lead to more fluid, collaborative environments. And while we often replicate our parents' gender-role assumptions, it's important to remember that not all parents' habits or traditions are wrong for all couples.

See you tomorrow.

Day 14

First, as always, begin with your breathing exercises.

Now, using the work we've done thus far on touch and gender, I'd like you to continue to think about your childhood environment and how it contributed to your sexual development. In Dr. Aline Zoklbrod's thoughtful book *Sex Smart*, she examines how childhood shapes one's adult sexual life, and she divides home environments into the seven following types based on how sexual topics are handled:*

- **THE IDEAL ENVIRONMENT.** In this happy home, sexual curiosity is encouraged; questions about sex are answered with age-appropriate information, and privacy and independence are respected and actively cultivated.

- **THE PREDOMINANTLY NURTURING ENVIRONMENT.** This environment is similar to the Ideal Environment above, albeit with some glaring gaps. For instance, a parent or sibling suffers from intermittent periods of depression or illness, or a divorce and remarriage cause a break in the seamless functioning of the Ideal Environment.

- **THE EVASIVE ENVIRONMENT.** In this scenario, the parents generally avoid the subject of sex and foster an environment where asking about sexual matters is uncomfortable. This is often consistent with a family where the parents are not openly affectionate with each other, even if they are affectionate to their children.

- **THE PERMISSIVE ENVIRONMENT.** At the other end of the pendulum is the home where sex is discussed too openly, with parents providing too much information too soon. In such a home, parents generally share intimate information with their children about their own sex

---

* Dr. Zoklbrod bases her typology on previous work published by Bolton, F., L. Morris, and A. MacEachron. *Males at Risk: The Other Side of Child Sexual Abuse.* Newbury Park, Calif.: Sage Publications, Inc., 1989.

lives and actively encourage their children to experiment sexually at too young an age to appreciate the emotional and psychological consequences.

- **THE NEGATIVE ENVIRONMENT.** In such a home, non-marital sex is not merely avoided but treated as immoral, providing a fertile nesting ground for homophobia, misogyny, and sexual problems in later life, including fear of masturbation, inability to achieve orgasm in women, and premature ejaculation in men.

- **THE SEDUCTIVE ENVIRONMENT.** In this scenario, relationships between parents and children or siblings are not overtly sexual, but are tinged with an inappropriate level of sexuality, including the routine discussion of age-inappropriate sexual matters.

- **THE OVERTLY SEXUAL ENVIRONMENT, OR WHAT I WOULD TERM THE ABUSIVE ENVIRONMENT.** Characterized by inappropriate sexual contact between a parent and child. Just to be absolutely clear, this inappropriate contact *does* constitute sexual abuse, even if the child often doesn't recognize it as such, or blocks it out. Whether the abuse happens just once or occurs over an extended period of time, is inflicted by a member of the immediate family or extended family of friends and relatives, growing up in an overtly sexual home can inflict long-term damage that impedes the ability to engage in healthy adult sexual relationships. From fear of intimacy to anger to lack of desire to promiscuity, overcoming the legacy of growing up in an overtly sexual environment requires time, work, and professional counseling.

An Important Note on Trauma

Growing up in an overtly sexual environment is just one of the ways children experience sexual trauma. People who grew up in abusive environments (which may not have necessarily been sexually abusive) often experience anxiety, lack of trust, fear of touch, and other symptoms that affect their adult intimate relationships. Every year, millions of children in the United States are the victims of either direct or indirect domestic violence and have been hurt by a parent or watched a parent get hurt.

If you're in this situation, it's extremely likely that you might not have thought about the connection between the non-sexual trauma you may have experienced as a child and the sexual intimacy issues you may be dealing with in your adult relationships. Many people who suffer from sex addiction, or conversely have no sexual desire, often find that they came from backgrounds that inspired fear and anxiety in relation to intimacy. The relationships they witnessed around them inspired distrust and unease rather than comfort and security. Many people are not on the extreme ends of the spectrum but have difficulties with intimacy nonetheless. Other traumas, such as a sexual assault or rape or a non-sexual assault that occurred outside the home during childhood, can also create lifelong intimacy issues unless they were properly addressed with parental support, understanding, and family and individual therapy.

In the case of serious traumas, treatment simply falls outside the purview of this book, and I would recommend you see a qualified therapist. Instead use this section to think about the connections between past and present, and consider this as a starting point for talking to a professional and discussing your issues openly with your partner.

Can you pinpoint which of the above environments most resembles your own family upbringing? If you're not sure, a good way to identify the best match is to think about your attitudes toward masturbation: Do you feel good about masturbation and recognize it as a healthy part of your sexuality? Has it helped you to understand and explore your own sexuality? Did you feel comfortable discussing it with your parents? Were they welcoming of your questions, avoidant of your questions, or chastising? Were they too liberal in dispensing provocative information in a way that made you uncomfortable?

Now think about what kind of family your partner was raised in. Was it similar or very different? This may be a crucial starting point for understanding and working through key differences in your attitudes toward sexuality.

Write up your thoughts in your Detox Diary, specifically discussing where you think your family and your partner's family falls on the seven-level environmental scale discussed above. Afterward, see if you can determine what kind of home each of your parents grew up in, since the attitudes they inculcated in you were first modeled on their own childhoods. Then take a few deep breaths and decompress.

See you tomorrow.

Day 15

It's been a very intense few days, you're halfway through, and now it's time for a little ME time. I would suggest you go for a massage. You deserve one. Allow yourself to luxuriate in the sense of touch and all the feelings and memories it inspires. When you get home, write about the experience in your Detox Diary. What did you think about during the session? Was it relaxing? Arousing? Stimulating? Freeing? Anxiety-inducing? See if you can connect your feelings with some of the key issues that we discussed during the past few days. Think about how you respond to touch, how your parents responded to touch, and how you and your partner interact with each other with regard to non-sexual physical intimacy. Is physical affection always arousing to you? Or, on the contrary, is it never arousing, but only comforting? Or not even comforting, but unsettling? During the massage, did your massage therapist point out any areas on your body that were overly tense? If so, are these areas that might also be tense during intimate interactions with your partner? Are there parts of your body that are hands-off with your partner for one reason or another?

As an example, many of my female patients are uncomfortable with parts of their body that they think are flabby—such as buttocks, thighs, or stomach—and as a result don't like to be touched there.

Take a few deep breaths and decompress—and, of course, congratulate yourself on completing another crucial step on the road to sexual and emotional fulfillment. Remember, this may be a good time to connect and constructively communicate with your partner about the work you've been doing during the detox. Try talking about the home environment you grew up in and how it affected your sexual development.

See you tomorrow.

MODULE 4: PREVIOUS RELATIONSHIPS
Days 16 to 20

FORMATIVE FIRSTS

The French novelist Colette wrote of sex, "these pleasures we lightly call physical," suggesting that when we think of our erotic lives as essentially being physical we greatly underestimate the significance of other dimensions, from the psychological to the cultural. Sex is often *anything but* "just" physical. And while we may choose to treat our pleasures lightly, they rarely treat us lightly in return.

That said, I don't want to suggest that there isn't an important role for a sense of lightness in your sex life. I was recently reminded of this when working with a woman named Jenny, thirty-four, who was struggling to reintegrate sex into her life after dealing with the shock of discovering her husband's infidelity. Over the course of nearly a year of turmoil, she had made significant progress in forgiving and forging ahead, but she found that sex was often "still heartbreaking," a potent reminder of the betrayal she'd endured: "The sex part is still so hard. The intimacy is overwhelming. It's like my mind has forgiven him, but my body won't. I feel as if Paul's infidelity has been etched into my DNA. I just want sex to be fun again, like it was when we first met, like it was when I was a teenager, when sex wasn't even sex, but just holding hands, kissing and touching."

For Jenny, the main goal of her journey through the Detox was to try and find a sense of lightness again. And while it's easy in hindsight to romanticize our "formative firsts"—from holding hands to fondling to every tantalizing thing in between—very often these experiences were often anything but romantic. Adolescence, if you'll strain to recall, was fraught with the struggle to temper our impulses, to seem cool to the right crowd, and to separate ourselves from our parents, all the while fumbling through the trial-by-fire indoctrination into sexual maturity.

Conflicts notwithstanding, there was still for each of us a time before sex, a glorious moment of innocence when sex existed as hot desire and future potential, when many of us, like Michael, thirty-four, couldn't wait to grow up:

"As a teenager, I was in such a rush to have sex 'like a real man.' I wanted to 'hit a home-run,' like my older brother was always bragging about. But today, I'm so bored and disappointed by sex with my wife that I feel like I've hit more home runs than Babe Ruth. The game no longer holds any interest."

During the rejuvenation phase of this program, you will hopefully be enjoying the "thrill of the chaste," in which everything old is new again. But first we are going to continue our journey of self-reflection and focus on our previous relationships, looking back to adolescence and some of those activities we "lightly call physical."

Day 16

We're going to start today as we have the previous days by engaging in our breathing exercises. Now review the list below and number the activities chronologically as they unfolded in your sexual history (which may not be the same as the order below).

Try to remember the first time you engaged in that particular act and with whom it happened. Describe the accompanying sensations and feelings.

_____Holding hands
_____Light kissing
_____Heavy kissing
_____Touching (outside of clothing)
_____Touching (under clothing)

_____Bisexual/homosexual experiences

_____Oral sex (giving)

_____Oral sex (receiving)

_____Intercourse

Here's what some others have had to say in remembering their first forays into hot romance. Please read them and see if they stir up any memories and feelings of your own. Now write about your own "formative firsts" in each area in as much detail as you remember.

Now go back and reread the entries, rating them each in terms of how positive or negative the experience was using the following scale: amazing, very positive, somewhat positive, neutral, somewhat negative, very negative, disgusting. For example,

HOLDING HANDS: "I remember holding hands with a boy named Jim. I was in fifth grade and we were out on a class trip. We sat next to each other on the bus and held hands beneath our jackets on the way to the museum. It was totally charged. When we actually got to the museum, we had to be sneaky and furtive, or everyone would have made fun of us. Holding hands felt really taboo, and was more exciting than much of my adult sex life."

Liz rated this experience: very positive

LIGHT KISSING: "I remember light kissing with some guy named Greg, well, at least I think his name was Greg. *Bor*-ing. It was seventh grade and we were playing Spin the Bottle at someone's birthday party. There were way more girls than boys at the party, so if a girl landed on another girl you would spin again until you got a guy. I remember thinking to myself when my spin landed on a girl named Joy that she was really pretty and I would have liked to kiss her more than most of the guys in the circle. But that would have been totally 'gay' back then. So I ended up kissing Greg and it was sort of like kissing a deflated inner tube. There was no chemistry. Later, when we played Seven Minutes in Heaven, I ended up going into the closet with him, and he was all excited and mashed my lips. Fortunately, I've had better kisses since, but maybe that's why I started dating older guys who knew how to show a little tenderness."

Rachel rated this experience: neutral

HEAVY KISSING: "I French kissed with Frank, who was my eighth grade boyfriend. He was in tenth grade. We used to go back to his house because his mom was working so we had the house to ourselves. We'd lie next to each other and kiss and kiss. Those kisses were wet, sloppy, and totally scrumptious."

Delia rated this experience: very positive

TOUCHING (OUTSIDE OF CLOTHING): "I'd let John touch me on top of my shirt, but I wouldn't let him go under. I guess I was a prude. I finally I let him kiss my bra and cleavage, but no nipples. Well maybe some nipple— but no bare-breasted nipple. I wanted to do more, trust me, but I was afraid of going too quickly. I guess I was a typical Catholic girl. Totally sexed up, but guilty and afraid of the wrath of God (well, really the wrath of my mother)."

Jade rated this experience: somewhat positive

TOUCHING (UNDER CLOTHING): "When I finally did touch my first penis, it was sort of freaky. It was this guy Rodney, and it was amazing the way it throbbed and slithered. Almost as soon as I touched it, he had an orgasm, and his cum got all over my hand. It was sticky and wet, and he was really embarrassed and made all these excuses about normally being able to last longer. I didn't know what to say, but as freaky as it was it felt really good to get a guy off like that. It was like proof of his sexual attraction to me. For a while, my relationship with Rodney was very one-sided; I'd touch him, but wouldn't let him touch me. But honestly I couldn't take it anymore, and there were plenty of other girls who were doing lots more, so I finally gave in. It seemed stupid to hold out, and I guessed I turned a corner with Rodney. When he first touched me down there, he made a comment about how wet I was, and I got really embarrassed. Even when he said what a turn-on it was, I was still uncomfortable. Now that I think about it, I'm sure that's part of why I was always uncomfortable getting oral sex from a guy for so long. It just felt so unhygienic, even though I know it's natural. I guess I didn't believe that it was really a turn-on."

Marcy rated this experience: somewhat negative

ORAL SEX (GIVING): "I gave Todd a blowjob, because, well, everyone else was doing it and I didn't want to be left out. And I also wasn't ready to have sex, so a blowjob seemed like a compromise. I didn't want him to think I was a tease. I was all prepared with my 'signature techniques,' but it didn't go as planned. He rammed my mouth a lot, and then held my head as he came. It was disgusting, like he had raped my mouth. I know that's strong language, but it took me years to actually enjoy giving head, and I was always worried about guys wanting to deep-throat me or force me to swallow. Today I love giving head and I think it's super-intimate, but when I think back to Todd it made me feel like I had been abused."

Mary rated this experience: disgusting

INTERCOURSE: I have not included any anecdotes about intercourse, as it is relevant to tomorrow's exercise. So for now, just note the placement of intercourse in your sequence of formative firsts, but hold off on writing about it.

BISEXUAL/HOMOSEXUAL EXPERIENCES: "In graduate school, my boyfriend really wanted to have a threesome, and I had always thought that I had a bisexual side. I used to masturbate about touching and being touched by a woman, so I thought it might be fun. What can I say? It wasn't. After watching my boyfriend have sex with another woman, I just couldn't respect the relationship any more. Some core trust had been violated. Maybe that's prudish, but after that I decided that some fantasies are best not shared or realized.

Tanya rated this experience: very negative

ORAL SEX (RECEIVING) "Getting satisfying oral sex from a guy didn't happen until I was in my late twenties. I think I was really lucky, because Bill knew what he was doing and he made me feel really good, and for a little while we were in love with each other. At first, I didn't know what he was doing and I was like, Ummm okay . . . actually one or two guys had tried in the past, but I really felt like I was someone who just didn't like it, and that guys didn't like it either. But Bill was loving and gentle and I had an amazing orgasm. Not only was Bill a first on the receiving side, but he also created a whole environment of trust around oral sex. I was able to tell him about some of my past negative experiences, and he was really supportive. My husband is lucky in that by the time we met I had really worked through so many issues and learned how to trust and enjoy sex."

Mindy rated this experience: amazing

Now tally your list: Are there more positives than negatives? Do you, like many of the people quoted, see any connections between how much your first experience with a particular activity may have colored your feelings about engaging in that activity to this day? If you labeled an experience "disgusting" or "very negative," are you still struggling to overcome negative feelings and anxiety?

While the power of formative firsts *can* be undone, they still play an important role in our sexual development and how our attitudes, likes, and dislikes are formed. In rereading the experiences you recalled above, how do you think they were affected by the kind of home you grew up in? For instance, if you were raised in a very religious home or what we termed a Negative Environment, how did this affect your formative firsts? Have you ever discussed your formative firsts with your partner? Are you familiar with his or her firsts?

Take a few deep breaths and decompress.

As always, see you tomorrow.

Day 17

Oh virginity, virginity, when you leave me, where do you go?

—SAPPHO, 600 B.C.

The cultural significance we place on losing one's virginity is so over-played, in my estimation, that this "first" often overrides all the others in our memories (not because it is inherently more significant, but because we have grown up with such emphasis placed on this one particular area of sexuality). In writing about your own loss of virginity, I'd like you to think about not only what happened, but what it meant to you, what you were expecting and why. In order to help gain some perspective, I'd like you to write about it as if it's a scene you're watching, using the third person "he" and "she" as a way of seeing it more clearly and with keener detachment.

As an example, Jenny (the same thirty-four-year-old from yesterday who grappled with her husband Paul's infidelity) wrote the following:

"It's prom night, and she enters the motel room with her date. He has a bottle of Jack Daniels they are both swigging from. They are drunk, he more than she. They kiss, but not for very long. He starts to take off her party dress. He compliments her constantly and tells her how sexy she is. She avoids prolonged kisses by going to work on his pants. She pushes him onto the bed and removes his pants. He closes his eyes, as though expecting her to go down on him, which she does. After a few moments, he opens his eyes, sits up, and tries to pull her toward him for a kiss. Instead she jumps off the bed and goes into her purse and removes a condom. She hands him the condom while she removes what is left of her clothing. They are both naked. He gets on top and kisses her as he penetrates her. He seems to be overwhelmed with excitement, as he gets more and more vigorous in his thrusting. He doesn't notice that she's staring at the ceiling, and that she is in pain as he thrusts harder and harder. As he moans, she starts to moan. He comes and collapses on top of her. She stares at the ceiling."

Now write about what was going on beneath the surface from the inside looking out: all the feelings, experiences, and expectations.

In Jenny's case, she wrote of the same experience:

"I was so excited. I thought it was going to be the hottest night of my life. And for a while it was: all the anticipation and dancing all night and knowing we were going to be doing what we were going to be doing. But Jerry didn't even touch me. He just *did* me. What did I learn from it? Intercourse was better for men than it was for women."

For many people, the loss of virginity is perhaps the most formative of "formative firsts," and alas, rarely meets our pre-experience expectations. In fact, many patients have told me they'd prefer to forget the whole thing. But it's important to remember and reflect. Maybe losing your virginity was one of those experiences where you were fortunate enough to have entered into it with reasonable expectations and where you had built enough trust and love with your partner to be able to say how you were feeling and help control the interaction, instead of feeling helpless and overpowered by it. For many, however, it *is* a loss in the truest sense of the word. Over time, many of us learn to operate out of this deficit, this vacuum in which we bury our disappointments, and we start to take the sense of disconnection for granted, to the point where we don't even notice it anymore. It's something we come to expect from sex: disappointment. It's like a scar that has faded with time, one that we no longer notice.

Now repeat the above exercise, but this time write about it as you imagined it might have been, like a scene in a romantic or even pornographic film, as you hoped it would enfold.

At the end of the day, I want you to read these two sets of scenarios back to back, first what actually happened, and second, what you had *hoped* your first sexual experience would be like. How does it make you feel? Sad? Amused? Disappointed? Does that sense of disappointment follow you to this day? Has it become a defining characteristic of subsequent sexual experiences? Gather up a few key words and images to symbolize important issues and memories we explored today—maybe, like Jenny, a picture from your prom. Then take a few deep breaths and decompress.

See you tomorrow.

Day 18

Begin the day with your breathing exercises.

Today, we will examine the qualities that comprise our "relationship dreams."

To begin, read through the following list of statements in its entirety. Then go back over it and circle nine statements that you consider most important with regard to your existing partner and that represent your relationship dreams:

1. I want my partner to show me how hot he or she finds me without my having to ask him or her.

2. I want my partner to ache with desire for me.

3. I want my partner to rip my clothes off and do me on the kitchen counter.

4. I want to writhe with anticipation over a romantic dinner for two.

5. I want my partner to talk dirty to me and make me wait until I'm ready to beg.

6. I want to have crazy knock-down, drag-out sex with my partner until we both pass out.

7. I want my partner to seduce me.

8. I want my partner to want to do things with/to me in bed that he or she never did with anyone else before.

9. I want my pulse to race when my partner touches me.

10. I want to get turned on by just the thought of having sex with my partner.

11. I want my partner to be desperate at the thought of us breaking up.

12. I want my partner to be jealous of other men or women.

13. I want my partner to want to spend more time with me.

14. I want my partner to tell me that I'm the best lover he or she ever had.

15. I want there to be no secrets between us.

16. I want my partner to promise we'll be together forever.

17. I want my partner to say I'm the love of his or her life.

18. I want my partner to send me love letters, buy me little gifts, and leave little love notes on the refrigerator.

19. I want my partner to swear he or she will never love someone else.

20. I want my partner to be so content he or she can't even fantasize about another woman or man.

21. I want my partner to make me laugh.

22. I want to have great conversations with my partner and never get bored.

23. I want my partner to stand by me through good times and bad.

24. I want my partner to be trustworthy, loyal, and truthful.

25. I want my partner to know how I'd react to something without having to ask.

26. I want my partner to remember anniversaries, birthdays, and other important occasions.

27. I want my partner to really like my friends and family.

√ **28.** I want my partner to be open to change.

⟨ **29.** I want my partner to respect me and be supportive of my decisions

30. I want my partner to grow old with me.

Look over the nine statements you selected:

FOR EVERY STATEMENT FROM 1–10 that you selected, add one point.
FOR EVERY STATEMENT FROM 11–20 that you selected, add two points.
FOR EVERY STATEMENT FROM 21–30 that you selected, add three points.

If you scored under 15, your relationship dreams are largely defined by desire, which may be something you desperately long for in your love life. If you scored between 15 and 24, your relationship dreams are dominated by thoughts of romantic love. Perhaps there's still a strong component of desire in your relationship, but you are in search of deeper emotional connections and affirmations of intimacy. If you scored over 24, your relationship dreams lie in the attachment phase. You long for a sense of safety and security for the most part.

In my experience, not only do all long-lasting, satisfying relationships progress through all three stages—desire, romantic love, and attachment—but those relationships that survive the test of time are able to hold onto aspects of each dimension, and hopefully your choices of relationship dreams represent the entire spectrum.

Next I want you to do the same exercise, but this time, answer from your partner's point of view. Now tally up the results. Were they similar or different? Do you think you're both on the same page in terms of your relationship dreams or are there striking differences in your relationship priorities and point of view?

Take a few deep breaths and decompress.

See you tomorrow.

Day 19

We will begin, as always, with our breathing exercises, writing down thoughts and feelings.

Today, we'll think back on our previous sexual experiences and the people we shared them with. Were the majority based on lust? Romantic love? Attachment? Or something else, like a sense of obligation?

After determining which category they fall under, list them under three columns (desire, romantic love, and attachment) in your Detox Diary.

What do your columns tell you? Do they have roughly equal numbers of past lovers in each, or is one column weighted more heavily than the others?

If the majority of your sexual experiences were desire-based, chances are you are a thrill-seeker or, in other words, you crave sexual excitement, often at the expense of long-term intimacy.

If they were largely based on romantic love, perhaps you still want sexual excitement and passion, but you also relish the thought of romance and something that can last forever.

If they mostly fell under the last category of attachment, you may be more driven by the need for security rather than sexual passion. What you want most is someone to grow old with and share your life with, rather than the thrill of lusty newness.

Beyond the three categories, are there any others you'd like to add? Of your previous sexual relationships, how many have straddled all three categories? Do you ever think back nostalgically on past loves? If so, which category do they fall into? In my clinical experience, it's perfectly natural to think about past lovers and exes (sometimes we even call out their names at the most indelicate times), or to suddenly find yourself reflecting upon someone that you hadn't thought about in ages. That doesn't mean you miss them or want to get back together with them, but it might tell you something about what you're missing or wanting out of your present relationship. By knowing which category an ex falls into (desire, romantic love, attachment), it might help you to understand the gaps you need to fill in the present.

Take a few breaths and decompress.

See you tomorrow.

Day 20

Today you'll enjoy another stint of ME time. Go to a spot you consider romantic, someplace that reawakens the surges of arousal and if possible takes you back to a time when you were first falling in love with your current partner. Spend some time sitting quietly to reflect on your thoughts and memories. Try to remember what you felt then, how excited you were, how much you wanted him/her to feel the same way. Try to recall the first time you remember thinking this could be "the one." Then think about where you are in the relationship now. Has it met at least some of your initial expectations? How has the relationship followed patterns similar to those from your past, ranging from past romantic partners to the relationships you saw in your childhood home? What good feelings can you bring home with you and potentially share with your partner?

Take a few deep breaths and decompress. And congratulate yourself on the completion of another phase toward sexual and emotional fulfillment. You're almost there. Remember, the end of the module may also be a good time to connect with your partner and constructively communicate about the work you've been doing. Try having a conversation about your formative firsts.

See you tomorrow.

MODULE 5: NAVIGATING YOUR LOVE MAP
Days 21 to 25

In this module we're going to continue our examination of your love map, which is the unique erotic fingerprint that drives your turn-ons and turn-offs, your sexual fantasies and fears. Living in a culture in which we are persistently bombarded with images of sex, it's often hard to filter out external noise so we can understand our own internal needs and desires—or, in other words, what turns us on from the inside rather than what we think *ought* to turn us on based on what we see outside. Rather than doing the hard and time-consuming work of looking within ourselves, most of us simply adopt the cookie-cutter images and sexual fantasies that we've grown up with. By understanding our unique love maps, however, we can isolate all the negative and positive experiences and feelings that have taken root in our libidos and figure out what's working for us and what's not, what is healthy and what is damaging, what is junk food and what is nutritious for our bodies and our minds. We can then eliminate the empty calories and toxins and build healthier paths toward lasting emotional and sexual fulfillment. We can learn to perceive ourselves as sexy based on who we are, not who we think we're supposed to be.

One of the best ways to understand what makes us tick sexually is to reflect on erotically memorable experiences from the past and our early fantasies, especially those that have survived in some measure over time and form a core sense of erotic identity.

As we undertake the following exercises, it is important to bear in mind that—unlike erotically memorable experiences that actually happened—our fantasies are not limited by the boundaries of reality, so they tap into areas that are often primal, unconscious, taboo, and lurking in the recesses of our psyche. Many of us feel unnerved by our own fantasies, and all of us have comfort zones in terms of how far we will let our imaginations wander. At first blush, our fantasies often seem to sit in stark contrast to the moral and societal values with which we were raised. For this reason, we tend to self-censor and repress them instead of letting our fantasies breathe and flourish.

In truth, however, they can help us identify key issues and dynamics we have grappled with from childhood onward. As a first step to knowing ourselves, it's important to do your best to free, rather than censor, the images and thoughts that truly turn you on.

Day 21

As always, please begin with your breathing exercises.

YOUR EROTIC MEMORIES

Today you're going to describe your most erotically memorable experience (or experiences.) Remember, I said erotically memorable, not necessarily *sexually* memorable. By that I mean that maybe the experience didn't actually involve sex, or orgasm, or only involved sexual interaction up to a point. Maybe a strong flirtation was your most erotically memorable experience, or an intense sense of sexual anticipation. Maybe it was a smoldering passion that was highly charged but sexually unrequited. If you feel you haven't had an erotically memorable experience, focus on a time when you felt an almost overwhelming pull of attraction and/or desire, something that seemed to come up in your fantasies time and again. Or maybe it was a scene in a movie or a passage in a book that left an indelible stamp on your sexual psyche.

Feel free to explore as many erotically memorable experiences as you like, but try to start out with an experience that really stands out in your mind, one in which you felt fully engaged in the moment.

As an example, Arthur, a recently engaged commodities trader in his mid-thirties, had always been a serial monogamist, dating a woman for a year or two at a time and then breaking up. In between his relationships, however, when he found himself lonely and horny, there was always one woman he could phone for some fun: Melissa.

Whether she happened to be in a relationship or not, Melissa made herself available to hang out with Arthur whenever he called. Arthur suspected that Melissa's feelings for him ran deeper than his for her, so his encounters were often fraught with guilt and ambivalence, which only heightened his arousal. Knowing he was, to a certain extent, using her for sex was a potent turn-on, especially considering that all of his other sexual experiences had been bound up in romantic relationships with girlfriends that were sexually tamer. "I'd get lonely and horny and I'd call Melissa up. She was always willing to come over. I didn't care that her readiness meant that she probably genuinely liked me. My loneliness and lust overshadowed any feelings of empathy or compassion. In fact it gave me a greater freedom; I didn't worry about pleasing her, or care about being tender or cuddly afterward. I could just be me, and explore a side of me that rarely had an outlet. This gave Melissa an intense erotic hold over me, which I guess we both knew and understood on some level, because the sex had a strong element of anger that ran though it: She was angry that I would never love her, and I was angry that I had to have her. It was exhilarating, remorseful, skin-scratching, flesh-grabbing, and all-consuming."

Arthur described his most memorable erotic experience with Melissa as follows: (Please keep in mind that this represents one man's particular experience, and I selected Arthur's memory because its intensity and clarity lends itself well to dissection and analysis. But everyone's experiences are different, and one person's sense of "erotically memorable" may be vastly dissimilar to another's. A turn-on to one person may be a turn-off to another, so please try not to judge Arthur's experience or to think of it as representative of everyone—that's the point: It stems from his unique love map.)

"One Sunday afternoon, Melissa and I met for an afternoon coffee at an outdoor cafe. I had just gone through an intense break-up, and hadn't seen or talked to Melissa in over two years. It was spring, but still a little cool, and she showed up wearing a miniskirt and thin sweater that kept sliding off her shoulder as we chatted. She wasn't pretty, but she was sexy as hell. She was very bold, and our encounters were always unrestrained and animalistic. With Melissa, the sexual anticipation was always intense, but I found myself wanting to get away from her almost as soon as we were finished. Knowing I was only interested in the sex and that it wouldn't go any further allowed me to let go in an unbridled way.

"On this particular occasion as we were leaving the cafe to take a walk, it started to rain. Melissa's studio apartment was only a few blocks away, so we made a mad dash to her place. I had never been there before: So this time I was on her ground. By the time we got there, we were both soaking and shivering, but I also felt tremendously alive. It might as well have been an electrical storm, that's how energized I felt.

"She told me to take a shower while she put my clothes in the dryer. When I was done, I put on the only towel available, which was so skimpy it barely tied around my waist. I came out of the bathroom with a hard-on that was impossible to conceal, expecting her to be similarly un-clad. Our encounters were always sex-based, so I was surprised that while I had been in the shower, Melissa had changed into jeans and a black turtleneck. As she stared at me, I felt sort of embarrassed. I tried to say something about it not being fair, but before I could finish my sentence she had yanked off the towel and stared me down. She gave me a look that let me know that she was definitely in charge. I felt naked, and sort of humiliated, but also really turned on. She pushed me down onto the futon and took total control. No kissing, no touching. Whenever I tried to kiss her, or undress her, or do something *to her*, she wouldn't let me. She also touched areas of my butt that no woman had ever gone near—even her, in our earlier wild forays. It was totally new, and it sent me over the top. I couldn't hold back as hard as I tried, and she encouraged me to come. When it was all over, I was completely naked and she was still dressed, holding me across her. It's funny, after that experience, I didn't want to leave. It was the first time ever I wanted to stay and hold her and be held by her, but she was up and in the bathroom before I had even recovered from my orgasm. That was the last time I ever saw her."

In a general conversation with Arthur about what made this experience particularly memorable, he said it had to do with feeling overwhelmed and out of control. As Arthur attested, "Normally, my hookups with Melissa happened on my terms, in my apartment, with me leading, but this time she was in control. I was naked and completely vulnerable, which is something I never felt with any woman during sex." Arthur's sense of vulnerability and powerlessness was enhanced by Melissa touching him in areas that he considered taboo, which offered new physical sensations to heighten the emotional and mental dimensions. What also made Arthur's experience erotically memorable was his rare loss of ejaculatory control and the liberating sense of being able to submit and surrender to someone else's touch. All this left him feeling "vulnerable, amped up, and sexually alive."

Now, write about your own erotically memorable experience in as much detail as you can. After you're done, answer the following questions:

1. When you think about the experience, does it still turn you on? *For Arthur, the answer is a resounding yes! Melissa still factors into his masturbation fantasies on a regular basis, and he sometimes fantasizes about her during sex when he's bored.*

2. Did any part of your memorable experience feel taboo, and how did that aspect make you feel? *For Arthur, it was the anal stimulation, which, although very light, was a totally new sensation.*

3. Were there any negative aspects that increased your resistance and made submitting to the moment that much more intense? *For Arthur, it was knowing that Melissa had feelings for him and that he was using her.*

4. How would you describe the major theme of this experience? *For Arthur, it was submitting and ultimately surrendering to someone else's control.*

5. Have you tried to incorporate these themes into your sexual experiences with other partners or your existing partner? *For Arthur, the*

answer was no. He was always too worried about his other lovers judging him as weak to get past the initial embarrassment of asking.

6. Can you see a connection between the theme of this experience and other areas of your life, past and present? *For Arthur, having a high-pressure job made losing control all the more liberating. In addition, he'd grown up in a large family and taken care of his younger siblings, resulting in an overweening sense of responsibility. As he stated, "In every relationship, I've been a caregiver. Except with Melissa."*

7. Did you have fantasies about this particular theme before the actual erotic encounter? What was going on in your life at the time? *For Arthur, yes, he had lightly fantasized about being dominated. Arthur said the fantasies had begun during puberty when he'd fantasized about his babysitter forcing him to pleasure her.*

8. Does fantasizing about this make you feel good or ashamed? How have your fantasies about this kind of experience evolved or changed over the years? *Arthur says he no longer feels ashamed, although it used to make him feel that way. He was ashamed at wanting to be dominated, but also ashamed at using Melissa as well as at the uncontrollable nature of his desire for her. He has grown more comfortable fantasizing about submission, often thinking about being tied up, teased, and forced to beg for release. He also enjoys Internet porn sites that feature women dominating men.*

9. Do you wish you could incorporate this fantasy into sex with your current partner? *For Arthur, the answer had always been "yes, but . . ." He did get off on the idea of his girlfriend dominating him, but because she frequently commented that she found male weakness a total turn-off, he never mentioned it.*

10. Is there anything else about this erotically memorable experience, and its core themes, that stand out as being worthy of exploration? Have you ever thought about these themes before? If you had a discussion with your partner about this experience and its themes,

how would he or she respond? With interest? Jealousy? Excitement? Repulsion? Can you envision using these themes to create a new erotically memorable experience with your partner?

If you'd like to explore your erotically memorable experiences further, I strongly encourage you to read *The Erotic Mind: Unlocking the Inner Sources of Passion and Fulfillment* by Jack Morin, Ph.D.

See you tomorrow.

Day 22

Start with your breathing exercises. Go back and reread what you wrote yesterday. Does it bring up any new memories, erotic fantasies, or desires or connections to the past? If so, write them down.

WHAT TURNS YOU ON?

Today, you will be paying extra attention to the external triggers that turn you on. When do you have sexual thoughts or fantasies during the day? What triggers them? Is it seeing someone who reminds you of an old lover, for example, or seeing couples holding hands or kissing? Is it making eye contact with a stranger on the train or brushing by someone at rush hour? Is there someone at your job who secretly forms the basis of your fantasies? Are you the type that thinks about sex a hundred times a day, or can a day pass with nary a sexual thought?

Instead of blocking these instances out, I want you to think about them. Let your mind wander. What kind of fantasies do you have? Do they relate to the erotic memory you wrote about yesterday? Are there other themes that consistently arise? Also, think about what and who turns you off and why. Are there certain sounds or smells that turn you off or on? Are you a visual person, or do you respond more to sound or scent? Think about these things as you go through the day. Take notes as often as you can. Then, when you get home in the evening, make a list of five to ten things that turned you on and five to ten things that turned you off during the course of the day. Are you surprised at any of the things in your list of turn-ons and turn-offs?

As an example, Erin, twenty-nine, considered herself a person who never thinks about sex. And yet, when she made her list during the day she was surprised that she thought about sex way more than she had previously realized. In particular, she noticed that lots of different smells turned her on—a colleague's cologne, a coat hanging on a hook next to hers, even the smell of a new book—and didn't necessarily make her think of sex, or want to have sex, but gave her a sense of erotic stirring.

See you tomorrow.

Day 23

As usual, begin today's session with your breathing exercises and a little Detox Diary journaling. If you have any new thoughts or connections that have been awakened during the last few days of thinking about past erotic memories, be sure to note them as well.

LIFE IS JUST A FANTASY

Today, we will be focusing on something that's come up quite a few times over the last few days: fantasy. Most people have at least one or more recurring fantasies that consistently turn them on. For some, a fantasy will be related to an experience from the past or someone they know. For others, it's rooted in scenarios involving specific themes, such as being tied up, being watched, or having an anonymous encounter with a stranger. Often, we have no idea where they come from or precisely when they seized hold of our imaginations. For this very reason, they offer a vital window into the construction of our love map. Unlike erotically memorable experiences, which have their roots in a clear moment of time, fantasies often stem from a place in our psyches that is anything but clear.

As an example of the relationship between erotically memorable experiences and fantasies, Kate, a woman in her late twenties, described an erotically memorable episode in which her current boyfriend went down on her for the first time and gave her an orgasm. Kate had always had problems having orgasms during sex, and was uncomfortable with oral sex, saying that it made her feel too vulnerable and that she had been better at giving pleasure than receiving it. But her current boyfriend, Thomas, was very supportive and gentle and made her feel relaxed and loved, and Kate finally experienced her first very powerful orgasm with another person and her first ever via oral sex. For Kate, the orgasm was connected to feelings of love and tenderness and being able to trust someone enough to let go. In short, her erotically memorable experience originated in a sense of comfort, safety, and emotional intimacy.

But when it came to her fantasies, what was happening in Kate's head was very different than what was happening in her bed: Her sexual imagination was piqued by a sense of danger.

In your Detox Diary, please answer the following questions:

1. **DESCRIBE YOUR "FAVORITE" OR MOST RECURRING SEXUAL FANTASY.** For Kate, her fantasies often involved watching her boyfriend having sex with another woman.

2. **WHAT ARE THE ELEMENTS OF THE FANTASY THAT PARTICULARLY AROUSE YOU, THE ONES YOU REPLAY OVER AND OVER?** Kate said, "Well, I'm really turned on by the idea of watching another woman pleasure my boyfriend. In my fantasy, the woman will often do things that I'm not comfortable with, like submission and domination. Watching him come without knowing that I'm watching is also an incredible turn-on, or at least it is in my fantasies."

3. **HAVE YOU EVER SHARED YOUR FANTASY WITH YOUR PARTNER?** Kate said: "No. I'm afraid he'd think I want to have a threesome, and I don't want to plant any seeds. Plus we really just don't talk about sex that much."

4. **DO YOU USE THIS FANTASY TO AROUSE YOU DURING MASTURBATION AND PRIOR TO OR DURING SEX WITH YOUR PARTNER?** Kate said yes to both.

5. **WHERE DO YOU THINK THE SPECIFIC POWER OF THIS FANTASY COMES FROM?** Kate's fantasy allowed her to transform her anxieties and fears into strengths. In her fantasy, she is observing from a place of power, and she is free to pleasure herself and participate passively in the sexual encounter without the active pressure to perform.

6. **HOW HAS THIS FANTASY CHANGED OVER TIME?** For Kate the fantasy has changed recently: She switches places with the other woman, becoming the woman he is having sex with instead of watching from the sidelines.

7. **DOES YOUR FANTASY TROUBLE YOU IN ANY WAY?** Kate, fortunately, has never been troubled by her fantasy. (But this is not always, or even often, the case for many people, who find their fantasies to be a source of guilt and shame, particularly when these fantasies violate social codes and taboos: Sex with someone of the same gender, rape fantasies, and fantasies about anal sex are just a few of the areas in which people often experience ambivalence over their fantasies. Recognizing how you feel about your fantasies is a powerful first step toward letting them breathe.)

8. **DOES THE THEME OF THE FANTASY EMERGE IN OTHER PARTS OF YOUR LIFE?** Kate's not sure. She is a freelance journalist and aspiring novelist. She thinks of herself as someone who is able to observe and think about issues objectively, which has allowed her to become detached in other aspects of her life, especially in relationships with men. So, perhaps the watching and observing from the shadows that occurred in the fantasy was consistent with aspects of her life.

9. **DOES THE THEME OF THE FANTASY EMERGE IN CONNECTION TO YOUR CHILDHOOD?** In thinking about her childhood, Kate described an

environment that was unsupportive of her sexuality, in which a strong double standard separated how her brother engaged with women and how she was supposed to engage with men. In terms of how this related to her fantasy, she said, "I think it represented a big step when I was able to put my own face on the face of the woman in the fantasy having sex with my boyfriend, and I was no longer watching in the shadows, but actively participating. That sort of ownership of my sexuality and sense of confidence in myself just wasn't instilled in me growing up."

10. IS YOUR FANTASY SOMETHING YOU WOULD LIKE TO PLAY OUT IN REALITY? IF SO, WHAT CHANGES WOULD YOU NEED TO MAKE IN ORDER TO STAY WITHIN YOUR COMFORT ZONE? Kate said she wanted to be able to share her fantasies with her boyfriend. She wasn't sure she'd like to act them out or make them happen, "but it would be a real turn-on just to talk about them and feel like we were connected mentally. We have a very safe relationship, and that's very important to me, and I would never want to give up the sense of comfort that allows me to have orgasms, but now that I can have them, I'd like to build on that comfort and safety by adding a little danger and unpredictability."

Does thinking about your fantasy turn you on or leave you feeling ashamed or embarrassed? Does the thought of sharing it with your partner make you aroused or terrified? How well do you know your partner's turn-ons and turn-offs? Your fantasy life is a big part of your sexual identity. While relationships need to be built on a foundation of honesty, trust, and predictability, sexual desire thrives on an element of unpredictability and mystery, on a sense of danger, risk, and naughtiness. Knowing your love map means having an acute sense of your turn-ons and turn-offs, what's "taboo" and what's "to-be." Some of us are lights-on, some of us are lights-off, and when it comes to knowing and sharing our fantasies, we all need a dimmer switch. But the first step is being able to shine a light within so that you can see the terrain of your unique love map.

See you tomorrow.

Day 24

Begin with your breathing exercises, as usual, and quickly peruse your diary entries in the current module through today.

TESTING THE LIMITS

Today you are going to spend some time trying to understand the boundaries of your sexual comfort zone, and safely test its limits and parameters. We will begin by focusing on issues of guilt surrounding sexual desires and fantasies. Sexual guilt often manifests itself during arousal and often produces feelings of shame, anger, and anxiety. Did rereading any of the exercises over the last few days make you feel uncomfortable or ashamed?

Please answer the following questions in your Detox Diary:

1. When I have sexual fantasies,

   a. I allow myself to get excited.

   b. I feel a sense of shame and try to repress them.

2. My sexual fantasies

   a. Don't challenge my sexual orientation or gender.

   b. Make me wonder about my sexual orientation or gender.

3. After I fantasize,

   a. I feel relaxed and comfortable.

   b. I feel stressed or agitated.

4. If I shared my fantasies with my partner,

   a. It would bring us closer together.

   b. I'm pretty sure he or she would find me weird or perverted.

5. When I get sexually aroused,

 a. I allow myself to express my desire through masturbation or with my partner.

 b. I try to block it out and hope my partner doesn't notice.

6. My sexual fantasies

 a. Don't challenge my religious or moral values.

 b. Do challenge my religious or moral values.

7. Kinky sex

 a. Is awesome, provided it's consensual.

 b. Is a sign that there's something emotionally lacking.

8. Use of pornography, erotic literature, and sex toys in a relationship

 a. Can be fun and creative.

 b. Means there is something wrong or missing.

9. When I have a fantasy that is too extreme,

 a. I recognize it's just that—a fantasy—and allow myself to enjoy it.

 b. I try to repress it.

10. If I fantasize during sex with my partner,

 a. I let myself do it.

 b. I feel bad about it and try to block it out.

Take a look over the results of your questionnaire. Did you select more than two responses from the B category? If so, you might have more sexual guilt than you previously thought. Would you characterize yourself as someone who gives their fantasies free reign and mentally enjoys them, or do your fantasies create a sense of guilt and ambivalence? Sexual guilt can be an extreme source of turmoil. The goal is to understand that turmoil, where it came from and why it occurs, and ultimately transform that negative energy into a positive one that stimulates sexual desire and fantasy, both alone and with a partner. If you feel that sexual guilt is crippling you, I implore you to go to the website for the American Association of Sexuality Educators, Counselors, and Therapists at www.aasect.org and get in touch with a qualified professional in your area. Sex therapy does not have to be an ongoing commitment, and sometimes even a single session can mean the difference between finding an empathetic ear and living a life of quiet desperation.

LET'S CONTINUE TO EXPLORE YOUR LOVE MAP

We're going to explore some broad types of fantasy that appeal to both men and women. In my clinical experience I've found that, when it comes to fantasy, men and women are more alike than they are different. In fact, in one survey I conducted with people who signed up to participate in anonymous surveys on my website, I asked men and women to submit a brief sexual fantasy. I then removed all gender references and asked another group to select which they thought had been written by men and which by women. In most cases, people could not tell whether the fantasies had originated with men or women, and often guessed mistakenly, a result that illuminated the general similarities between the sexes.

In navigating your love map, I would like you to reflect on the four "poles of desire": voyeurism, exhibitionism, domination, and submission. Let's explore these four poles in more detail:

Exhibitionism: Does the idea of being watched—by a lover, by a stranger—turn you on? Have you ever engaged in any acts of exhibitionism—from skinny-dipping to having loud sex to having sex outdoors to making a sex tape? What would be an exhibitionistic fantasy that, while pushing your comfort zone, you might do under the right circumstances? What would be an exhibitionistic fantasy that turns you on, but one that you would never want to act out?

What's your safe, sexy danger zone? Write down one exhibitionistic turn-on and one turn-off. As an example, Jenna was turned on by the idea of a quickie in the stairwell with her boyfriend, but turned off by the idea of having a threesome with another woman and being watched by her boyfriend.

Voyeurism: Do you like to watch? If you looked outside your window and saw two people having sex in a window across the way, would you avert your eyes or reach for binoculars? Do you have a fantasy of watching your lover and another get it on together? What are some of your voyeuristic fantasies? Are there any you'd like to explore?

What's your safe, sexy danger zone? Write down one voyeuristic turn-on and one turn-off. As an example, Richard was extremely turned on by the idea of watching his wife masturbate for him and "seeing how she does it," but was turned off by the idea of making a sex tape.

Domination and Submission: From ropes and a smack on the fanny to sex in positions that exploit the helplessness of your lover, where do your tastes lie?

What's your safe, sexy danger zone? Write down one domination-based turn-on and one turn-off. As an example, Kristine was turned on by the idea of tying up her husband and teasing and tantalizing him into submission with oral sex, but was turned off by the idea of any sort of spanking or violence.

What's your safe, sexy danger zone? Write down one submission-based turn-on and one turn-off. As an example, Matthew was turned on by the idea of being tied up and spanked by his live-in girlfriend, but was turned off by the idea of any sort of anal play.

At the end of the day, take some time to think about what fantasies you've explored in the past, and what you would want to try in the future. Then review what you wrote today. How does it make you feel? Turned on? Ashamed? Some combination of both? Can you envision creating a "sexy, safe danger zone" with your partner? Do you think he or she would be turned on by your fantasies or turned off?

See you tomorrow.

Day 25

Now it's time to enjoy a little ME time, something that will hopefully stimulate your fantasies. Maybe a trip to a sex toy shop—to just look or to buy—or maybe a walk around the park with a little erotic reading material. Make sure you think about all the issues and fantasies we've been exploring as you spend some time out in the world. Feel the pleasure of knowing you are watching and being watched. Indulge your fantasies in the safety of your interior thoughts, knowing they belong only to you, to be shared or not, at your discretion alone. Revel in being alone without feeling un-sexy.

Congratulate yourself on the completion of another crucial step on the road to sexual and emotional health and fulfillment. And remember, this may be a good time to connect and constructively communicate with your partner about the work you've been doing during the detox. As a start, pick up a couple of mainstream magazines and, thumbing through the photos, think about what you find sexy vs. unsexy.

See you tomorrow.

MODULE 6: THE HERE AND NOW
Days 26 to 30

In this last module, Days 26 through 30, we are going to focus on your current relationship. Some of you may be wondering how it's possible that we've come this far without delving too deeply into this subject; I purposefully waited until the end of the Detox because, in my experience, a current relationship is almost always the catalyst for seeking help or desiring change. And the intensity of the issues associated with the current relationship almost always overshadows everything else. The state of your current relationship is probably what brought you to this program, but as you've seen it's certainly not the whole picture. First I wanted to give you a chance to focus on *you*. Now let's look at your relationship.

Day 26

Begin with your breathing exercises. By now you should be associating these few minutes with a sense of calm and relaxation.

We begin the first day of the last module of our Sex Detox by examining the state of your relationship *outside* of the bedroom. As I said in the introduction, a satisfying sex life requires a strong relationship to support it, and there's an intense dynamic between what happens in the bedroom and what happens outside of it. We'll be looking at the hostility, resentment, and negative behavioral patterns that may be manifesting in your relationship. To that end, complete the following true or false questionnaire as honestly as possible:

1. Little arguments tend to escalate into bigger fights. True or False?

2. When we fight, we quickly get off subject and start arguing about other issues. True or False?

3. After we fight, one of us tends to hold a grudge. True or False?

4. An atmosphere of negativity and criticism frequently pervades our relationship. True or False?

5. My partner and I aren't very good at working our way through a fight and moving on. Neither "forgive" nor "forget" are in our relationship vocabulary. True or False?

6. When one of us does try to "repair" from a fight—by making a joke, apologizing, reaching out for physical contact—our efforts often fail. True or False?

7. One or both of us often goes to bed angry. True or False?

8. When it comes to things like chores or spending money, there are aspects of our relationship that are unfair or operate on a double standard. True or False?

9. I feel like I have to walk on eggshells around my partner and worry about provoking his/her temper. True or False?

10. I feel like my partner isn't loyal to me with his or her friends and family. True or False?

11. My partner and I don't share the same values or priorities. True or False?

12. My partner rarely makes me laugh. True or False?

13. My partner belittles me, dismisses me, storms off, and generally terminates rather than engages discussion. True or False?

14. When I do engage my partner, I am really afraid that he or she will overreact and get bent out of shape. True or False?

15. My relationship negatively impacts my self-esteem. True or False?

16. I've lost trust for my partner. True or False?

17. I feel like my partner is a complete mystery to me in some ways. True or False?

18. If I try to tell my partner how I'm feeling, he or she generally accuses me of being over-emotional or argumentative. True or False?

19. It just doesn't feel like we're on the same team. True or False?

20. I often don't even tell my partner what I'm thinking because I'm afraid of his or her reaction. True or False?

21. I think about breaking up, separating, or divorcing often. True or False?

22. I think I care about the relationship more than my partner does. True or False?

23. If we broke up, we'd probably both be a lot happier. True or False?

24. I find myself getting angry over little things. True or False?

25. I feel trapped in this relationship. True or False?

26. My friends and family worry about me and want me to be happier. True or False?

27. I feel like I can't breathe in this relationship. True or False?

28. This relationship isn't ever fun anymore. True or False?

29. When my partner tells me that he or she loves me it feels mechanical or phony. True or False?

30. I have become disillusioned and disappointed, and have lost respect for my partner and our relationship. True or False?

31. It's hard for me to empathize when my partner is upset. True or False?

32. When it comes to certain issues, like money or raising kids, I feel as if there's no way to find a center. True or False?

33. I don't really care if my partner succeeds unless it will benefit me directly. True or False?

34. I don't really care what my partner thinks. True or False?

35. I feel like my partner doesn't really know me. True or False?

36. I am happier away from my partner than I am with him or her. True or False?

37. We are bored with each other. True or False?

38. We live in separate worlds. True or False?

39. Even if we sleep in the same bed, I feel like I'm sleeping alone. True or False?

40. There's a lot of water under the bridge, maybe too much. True or False?

If you marked less than ten statements as true, you still have a lot of positive energy and good will to draw upon. More than likely, there's a relatively strong degree of trust in the relationship and an ability to work through your issues. There may be rough moments ahead, but they're not deal-breakers.

But if you marked more than ten statements, but fewer than twenty, as true? Well, you've got some serious work to do. If there's enough desire on both sides to compensate for prolonged periods of anger, distrust, and negativity, it can be done. But more than likely you've lost the romantic ideals and positive feelings about your partner that once fueled much of your relationship. It's been a case of lowered expectations and continually diminishing returns that have left you wary and unwilling to exert the effort to make things better, mostly because you've lost faith that they can be better. If you want it badly enough and you're willing to try to build new paths to each other, it's possible to bring your relationship back to a healthy place. But it will take time and effort.

If you marked more than twenty statements as true, the hard truth is that things may be reaching a point beyond repair. And in all honesty, I wouldn't recommend that you try to work things out without the help of serious relationship counseling. Chances are you're staying in the relationship out of fear, inertia, or for financial reasons, the sake of the children, or some such important reason. And settling for something for any of those reasons alone is not going to leave you feeling happy, proud, or fulfilled on any level. It's far more likely to be destructive—not just to you and your partner, but to everyone else around you.

What happens outside the bedroom affects what happens within those four walls. And it doesn't take too many "trues" to start affecting your sex life. However, as long as your list of trues is less than 50 percent it's my belief that sex can play a healing and rejuvenating role in your overall relationship.

But it's very possible that, for some of you, while the Detox has been a powerful way to reflect upon issues and to come to terms with your thoughts and feelings, with so many trues checked off on your list, you and your partner are simply not ready to approach sex with the right kind of attitude. This is something you need to think long and hard about—and, of course, you must think carefully about how my comments apply to you and your specific situation. They are guidelines to spark further consideration, not rules.

Take some time to review your findings. How do you feel? Was it what you expected? Are you relieved? Disappointed? Fearful? Regardless of what you scored, it's important to understand that good sex is not a cure-all. It can only make a relatively healthy relationship better by drawing you closer and making your intimate moments more enjoyable. But, if your relationship contains extremely high levels of emotional toxicity, then the Sex Detox may help you to develop a stronger foundation of sexual and emotional awareness and health, but it is unlikely it will be enough to rescue your current relationship, and I would personally be extremely suspect of any book that promises otherwise. You may need to take stronger action to be in the kind of relationship that produces a satisfying sex life.

How would your partner answer the questionnaire? Do you think you're feeling similarly or differently? If you're interested in seeking counseling, but unsure where to turn, there are organizations such as the American Association of Sexuality Educators, Counselors, and Therapists and The American Association of Marriage and Family Therapists that serve as gatekeepers to licensed, certified professionals. Both of these are available online at www.aasect.org and www.aamft.ortg, and truly, help is a mere click away.

See you tomorrow.

Day 27

Please begin with your deep breathing exercises.

As you continue I'd like you to reflect on the *connections* you make with your partner outside of the bedroom: connections that may not be explicitly sexual, but that create what I call "transferable" desire and contribute to lasting sexual desire and fulfilling sexual experiences. For example: non-sexual physical intimacy such as hugging and holding hands, laughing together or playing little pranks on each other, leaning into each other while you watch television, cleaning up together after a meal, sharing the day's events and genuinely listening, and so on. While these types of interactions and connections may not seem inherently sexual, they help to generate a reservoir of transferable desire and a greater disposition toward sexual desire.

To what degree does your relationship have a reserve of transferable desire, or to what extent are you stuck in a "non-transferable" relationship? Is it rare for you and your partner to have any sort of non-sexual physical intimacy? Are you living under the same roof but in different worlds? If you're in a non-transferable relationship, what are the challenges facing you to transform it into a transferable one? Take a few minutes to think about this, and write down anything that comes to mind.

Now that you've begun to think about transferable desire, we will continue by assessing your basic level of desire for your partner. Please ask yourself the following yes or no questions. Take your time and respond as honestly as possible.

1. Do you have feelings of sexual desire for your partner?

2. Do you think if you met your partner for the first time today, you would fall in love with him or her all over again?

3. Do you still find your partner sexually attractive?

4. When you go out to a social event with your partner, are you proud to be with him or her?

5. Are there little things about your partner that get you turned on? His or her scent for example, or a cute gesture or turn of phrase?

6. Do you have sexual thoughts about your partner during the day?

7. Does a sexy thought about your partner contribute to a desire to want to have sex with your partner?

8. Does the prospect of going out on a date night that's just the two of you make you happy?

9. If your sex life had to basically remain as-is for the next five years, would you be satisfied?

If you answered yes to at least five of the above questions, you're in decent shape, at least so far as basic sexual chemistry goes. If you answered no to more than five questions, your feelings of romantic attachment are likely dimming. While you may have the emotional basis to form a lasting friendship, you may not have the erotic connection to sustain a healthy and fulfilling sexual relationship. It's important to keep in mind that sometimes it's possible for someone to be tuned out of the relationship and their partner's emotional life, but still be turned on by them physically. This usually results in a relationship where the sex life is still intact, but lacks genuine emotional connection. For the relationship to flourish, you need to possess the potential for both emotional warmth and sexual attraction.

Please consider the following activities. How often do you engage in them on a weekly basis? Would your partner be likely to respond in the same way?

1. Hug/embrace
2. Hold hands
3. Kiss
4. Say "I love you"
5. Call during the day to say hi and check in
6. Compliment each other
7. Email each other
8. Eat meals together
9. Take time to really talk about each other's day
10. Do chores together
11. Go on date nights regularly
12. Watch favorite TV shows or read the newspaper together
13. Socialize with others together
14. Cultivate/participate in mutual hobbies/common interests
15. Go on vacations together

If you engage in at least twelve of these four times a week or more, you're definitely connected on an emotional level. If not, try to think about ways to increase the frequency of positive interactions in your daily life. You'll be surprised how easy it is once you get started.

Now consider some of these other activities, which are more directly linked to desire. On a weekly basis, how often do you do the following?

1. Kiss tenderly
2. Fool around without the expectation of immediate sex
3. Compliment/comment on each other's sexual attractiveness/sexiness
4. Call each other up during the day and flirt
5. Talk about sex/fantasies
6. Engage a sexual sense of humor/get bawdy with each other
7. Dress provocatively for each other's eyes only
8. Engage in playful exhibitionism
9. Engage sexually outside of the bedroom
10. Read erotic literature/watch erotic films together

If you engage in half of these activities or more at least once a week, you are still sexually connected and erotically charged. If not? Well, then, you're just like the vast majority of couples in long-term committed relationships. You might be happily committed, but you're in a sexual rut! Then again, chances are you knew that already or you wouldn't be reading this book.

So how do you get out of this rut? We're going to think about ways that you can integrate the above activities into your current daily routine, say to the tune of one activity per day. If it feels awkward or out of character—which is fairly likely—do it on your own terms. You don't have to parade around in a bra and g-string for your partner, or bulk up your biceps. If talking sexy on the phone seems a bit stilted given where you are in the non-dating game, try a slightly naughty email instead. Be creative. Do what is comfortable, but think about ways to modify the above list so that you can build at least one of these *general* suggestions into your daily routine.

Then take a few breaths and decompress.

See you tomorrow.

Day 28

As always, begin with your breathing exercises.

Today, we will be working on developing a healthier level of overall desire. When we are first falling in lust and/or love with someone, just the thought of them makes us jittery. But later, as we move through the relationship cycle into deeper attachment, this is generally replaced by a sense of comfort. That's when we have to do a little work in order to re-create that sense of newness that made it so hot at the beginning.

Getting back to that place of "newness" is what we're going to work on today.

First I want you to list as many things as you can recall about your partner that turned you on when you first met. Some of them may be no longer applicable—for example, maybe he or she was unavailable at the time and was thin, and now the two of you are married and he or she is overweight. No matter, write it all down and we'll worry about that later.

For instance, Sarah made a list about what first attracted her to her husband of ten years, Chris, as follows:

1. Incredibly articulate and well read
2. Slightly arrogant
3. Great tennis player
4. Lean and muscular with olive skin
5. Extremely ambitious and driven
6. Scathing sense of humor
7. Well-traveled
8. Loved Bergman movies
9. A Democrat
10. Baked croissants from scratch

Now think about which of your statements is still true. Sarah, for example, felt that Chris had gone from slightly arrogant to borderline obnoxious. Nonetheless, many of the items still held true. There were also a few new positive attributes she could add to the list. See if you can add new positives as well:

11. Wonderful, attentive father to their child
12. Mastered extensive repertoire of vegan dishes for her sake (even though he was a die-hard carnivore)
13. Willing to give her regular neck massages

There were also some negative attributes, of course. Find and add these to your list, as Sarah has below:

14. Absolute, utter slob
15. Talks back to the television during baseball games
16. Anti-social with her friends and family

Looking at your own list of positive and negative attributes, think about how the negatives have gotten in the way of experiencing the positives. For Sarah, the fact that Chris had become a total slob often impeded her ability to enjoy many of his other, finer attributes. While it would certainly be nice if our partners magically transformed themselves into our absolute ideals, chances are it ain't gonna happen. So try to imagine situations, for the time being, where the negative tendency or attribute might not come into play, or situations that bring out the positive.

When Sarah and Chris go out, the fact that he is a slob becomes less of an obstacle to her enjoyment of his company, since they are not in situations where he can be messy. But they rarely go out without their young son in tow, which Sarah finds just as stressful. By finding times to go out without their toddler and without the possibility that her husband will create a big heaping pile of mess—*and* while strategically avoiding places where a sports game might be playing that would elicit another of his unfortunate verbal tendencies—Sarah has been able to call upon the desire associated with these positive attributes rather than give sway to the negative ones.

When you are done, reread your lists. Think about the activities we discussed yesterday that create a state of transferable desire. Now create a short list of simple, achievable situations in which positive sentiment would prevail over negative sentiment and those activities might be given a chance to flourish. For Sarah it was more than just dinners out without her toddler in tow, it was also taking drives with Chris, shopping at Farmers markets, and cooking meals again together, going to museums again, or even just meeting up after work for a glass of wine before going home together. Think about how engaging in these activities makes you feel. Excited? Happy? Turned on, at least a little? If not, think about what's impeding those feelings.

See you tomorrow.

Day 29

Begin with your breathing exercises. You are almost at the end of the Detox—how does that make you feel?

It is the rule rather than the exception that virtually everyone I have worked with suffers from an issue, or grapples with an obstacle, that prevents them from having the sex they desire. Sometimes, as we have been discussing for the last few days, these problems are largely related to issues outside the bedroom, but oftentimes they happen during sex itself. Today we're going to go "under covers."

There are different phases to the process of sexual response:

- *Desire,* in which ones wants sexual intimacy;
- *Excitement* (also called *arousal*), in which blood flows to the genitals (vasocongestion) and sexual tension (myotonia) develops throughout the body;
- *Plateau,* in which one reaches a peak of sexual excitement prior to orgasm;
- *Orgasm,* in which sexual tension is released; and, finally
- *Resolution,* the period after orgasm in which the body returns to its pre-excitement state.

Obstacles to the process of sexual response can occur in any or all of the phases—and these obstacles can in turn trigger a cascade of reactions. As an example, sometimes a person can experience a strong sense of desire, but have difficulty maintaining arousal and having an orgasm. Conversely, sometimes a person can be slow to start and experience low desire, but once they're up and running they have no problems enjoying the full process of sexual response.

In men, common obstacles in the process of sexual response include low desire, rapid ejaculation, erectile disorder, anorgasmia (the inability to have an orgasm), and delayed ejaculation. In women low desire, inhibited arousal, anorgasmia, and pain during intercourse contribute to millions of unsatisfying sex acts daily.

These common obstacles can produce any one of an array of related behaviors. Some, like making the effort to communicate about the issue or working to find alternative sexual modes of expression, are positive. As an example, a man who suffers from rapid ejaculation might become more proficient at oral sex or using his hands or a vibrator to provide persistent clitoral stimulation to please a female partner.

But more often than not, these obstacles produce negative behaviors, or what I call "covers," which enable one to avoid the issue and steer around meaningful communication about it. As an example, a woman who suffers from inhibited arousal might fake it to avoid hurting her partner's feelings.

Now, I want you to think about your own and your partner's obstacles to sexual satisfaction and how you've learned to cope with them (if you have at all) or what covers you've put in place if not. Think about the extent to which it continues to be an impediment to your maximum enjoyment of sexual intimacy, and discuss this in your Detox Diary.

As an example, Mary, twenty-five, noted of her sex life with her twenty-eight-year-old fiancé, Henry, that she gets turned on and has lots of desire, but rarely has orgasms during sex. Instead, she fakes it, although Henry rarely asks and seems to just assume that if he's having an orgasm she must be as well. Mary has no problem having orgasms on her own, and frequently has to "finish herself off" in the bathroom after having sex.

Mary's inability to have an orgasm during sex manifests in both a positive behavior and a negative cover. The positive behavior is her take-charge attitude toward masturbation and her recognition that the problem isn't about her own sexuality, but her relationship. Her cover, however, is faking her orgasms, or not letting her fiancé know that she rarely experiences them during sex. Although both Mary and Henry would benefit from honest communication, Mary insists that she doesn't want to hurt Henry's feelings or wound his pride, so she withholds communication.

How could Mary and Henry ultimately circumnavigate their current pattern of behavior and create an alternate pathway to mutual satisfaction?

First, Mary would need to look back to her early years of sexual development to understand why she feels guilt about disappointing Henry regarding his presumed sexual prowess to give her orgasms. Next she would need to examine and retrace formative firsts and subsequent experiences that reinforced this tendency to fake it. Last, she would look at how that has culminated in the current form of the behavior. She would then create a new pattern of behavior by recognizing and rationally deciding against succumbing to the stereotypes she grew up with regarding the need to make a man feel virile and her belief that women were supposed to be satisfied by intercourse alone. She would search her memory banks for memories of having an orgasm with a partner that were positive. If none existed, she would create it fresh. She would visualize it and practice it until it became second nature, until it was hardwired into her sexual response patterns. And most important she would start to communicate with Henry constructively about how to change their sex scripts so that she was more orgasmic.

Now, take a few minutes to reflect upon the obstacles you and your partner may be experiencing, as well as the "covers" they produce. Go through the same process Mary did, considering the causes of these "obstacles" and the particular patterns and behaviors that underlie them. Then come up with alternate memories and associations that would validate or provide a starting point for a more positive pattern of behavior.

At the end of the day, reread what you've written and think about it.

How does it make you feel? Aroused? Eager to get started? More confident that you have the potential to change your behavior and re-appropriate the past to make it your own? The power is yours.

See you tomorrow.

Day 30

In the spirit of our final ME time session in this Sex Detox, I want you to take some time—as much or little as you need—to read through your entire Detox Diary. Go somewhere comfortable and relaxed: a park bench, the corner of a coffee shop. Don't worry if you can't get through the whole thing—even though the modules have officially ended, hopefully you'll still be treating yourself to a good deal more ME time down the line.

Think about what it means to truly be a "sexual person." When most people talk about being "sexual," they're usually thinking about sex in a very superficial way: They're referring to the number of sexual partners they've had in the past, or think being a sexual person means that they like to have sex a lot and need it often (usually more than their partner does), or that they simply love having orgasms. But being a sexual person is more than just liking sex. Being a sexual person means that you're willing and able to communicate proactively about sexual issues with your partner, that you're committed to the spirit of ongoing sexual creativity, that you sustain your sexual fitness and live a sexually healthy life, that you're aware of past experiences that may be impairing your full enjoyment of sex, that you have empathy for your partner and his or her issues, that you recognize that sexual desire ebbs and flows across the life cycle (both within yourself and within your relationship), and that sex changes. Being a sexual person also means that you're tuned in and turned on rather than tuned out and turned off, and that you're comfortable with your fantasies. Your "sexual history" is so much more than just the number of partners you've had. It's who you are and what you bring to those experiences. Your sexual history is the sense of self-esteem and self-respect you bring to your sex life. It's how you value your sexual identity and the expression, gratification, and growth of that identity. Your sexual history isn't just something that happened in the past. It's something that's happening right now. It's never too late to take ownership of your sexual history and to allow yourself to truly become a "sexual person."

As with the previous modules, this may be a good time to reconnect with your partner and share some of the work you've been doing. As a suggestion, go back to Day 28, page 110, and remind your partner of all the qualities that attracted you to him or her when you met. Congratulations. You've made it through the Detox. Like any fast, this one may have left you famished. But don't go off and blow it on a binge now! We're going to feed that massive appetite with healthy, tasty, and well-prepared "foods" that sate your unique hunger rather than quell your short-term cravings.

With that in mind, think about what you might like to see on the menu. You start your love feast tomorrow, so rest up and get ready for the rejuvenation phase that comes next.

7.

The Couples' Rejuvenation

Without frequent touch—for example, when mates are apart—the brain's dopamine and oxytocin circuits and receptors can feel starved. Couples may not realize how much they depend on each other's physical presence until they are separated for a while.

—DR. LOUANN BRIZENDINE, M.D.,
THE FEMALE BRAIN

Now that you've completed the Detox, it's time to connect the dots between past and future, mind and body, and translate thought into action. When people ask me about the relationship between the Detox and the rejuvenation plan I often use the analogy of going to see an allergist. Even if you know you're suffering from an allergic reaction, it's still often difficult to pinpoint the triggers. What an allergist does first is have you complete a detailed medical history that covers everything from lifestyle, diet, and habits to psychological stressors. Then he or she puts you on a diet to eliminate certain foods and pricks you with small amounts of toxins to narrow down the precise causes of the allergy.

One of the main goals of this program is to try to help you re-approach your relationship on a holistic level, with a renewed sense of hope. As a first step, we took sex off the table during the Detox. Now we are ready to re-introduce sex into your relationship. But much like dealing with an allergy, it's important to be sensitive to negative reactions you may experience along the way. Therefore, we'll be building your new "sex diet" through incremental activities and carefully considered steps that you can do at your own pace. Unlike the Detox, which followed a sequential thirty-day program, the Rejuvenation proceeds flexibly at a pace that is unique to your needs. For some it may take a matter of days, for others weeks, even months. The main point is to proceed in a manner that works for you through the following four stages:

1. Warming Up
2. Touching to Tune In
3. Touching to Turn On
4. Touching to Transcend

STAGE 1: WARMING UP

Though it may sound counterintuitive, your sexual Rejuvenation will begin outside the bedroom. We'll work our way back into the bedroom eventually, but for now we're going to get ourselves warmed up. Let's begin with a few basic exercises:

REVIEW THE ISSUES YOU EXPLORED IN YOUR DETOX DIARY WITH YOUR PART-
NER. Keeping in mind that your Detox Diary is private and for your eyes only, try to review some of the ways you believe your past has impacted your present and be sure to highlight the particular negative associations and memories you wish to be mindful of in moving forward. For instance, if you realized that you are somewhat inhibited about various aspects of sex owing to your early sexual experiences, let him or her know so you can work together toward creating more positive patterns of behavior together. In doing so, however, be sure to remember that when it comes to communicating about sex, there's often a gap between *what* we want to say and *how* we say it, and even the most innocuous of words can come off as confrontational. Criticism, expressed or perceived harshly, can be the sexual kiss of death.

CONVERSE IN A WAY THAT IS RELAXED AND SIDE BY SIDE, AS OPPOSED TO EYE TO EYE. When you're ready to talk to your partner, don't do so while sitting across from each other at a table staring into each other's eyes. In my experience, women are much better with direct eye contact than men, and men often respond defensively to eye contact, even when the tone of the conversation is peaceful. Anthropologists have long observed that women are face-to-face communicators, while men seem to prefer to be side by side. This means that women are much more comfortable with direct eye contact, which probably has a lot to do with the long history of maternal nursing, cuddling, and fawning over infants while staring lovingly into those big baby eyes. Men, on the other hand, find direct eye contact confrontational on an instinctive level. As Dr. Helen Fisher wrote in her remarkable book, *Why We Love,* "This response probably stems from men's ancestry. For many millennia men faced their enemies; they sat or walked side by side as they hunted game with their friends." So regardless of your gender, approach the conversation with your partner in a way that respects the differences in your communication styles.

MAKE SURE TO DISCUSS YOUR ISSUES IN TERMS OF YOURSELF AND NOT YOUR PARTNER. There will be plenty of opportunities down the line to discuss any issues you have with your partner's actions, but for now focus on setting the stage for constructive communication by conversing in terms of your wants, needs, and desires. Coming out of the Detox, your attitude should be one of confidence and empowerment. Hopefully you've gained a new appreciation for the complexity and multifaceted nature of sex. You've had a lot of time to think about the issues, and no doubt you have a lot to say. The main thing is to do so in the spirit of positive, mutually beneficial change. Rather than trying to get everything said in one conversation, or in one day, give yourself the time you need to do it in smaller manageable doses—an hour here, a half hour there. But do keep track of what you have said and what you need to say in order to move beyond the past into an open future. If it helps, work from your Detox Diary, devoting each day, or each week (depending on your pace), to a different module.

Take your partner on a guided tour of your detox experience. Or use the process of reORDERing as a roadmap for working and talking through the issue(s):

Observe (both the situation at hand with your partner and how outside influences may have shaped your behaviors); **R**ecognize (recurring patterns and what triggers them); **D**e-couple (your responses from those triggers, so you can manage those moments more smoothly); **E**ngage (in healthier behaviors), and **R**egulate yourself as you move forward with a new sense of awareness (realizing that you're not responsible for your partner's actions and reactions, but you are responsible for your own).

As an example, maybe you're in a sex rut and your libido is lower than your partner's. Take the time to **O**bserve the situation: how you got to this place and the implications for your relationship. Maybe your sexual health plays a role in your lack of desire. **R**ecognize the patterns that are emerging around the issue: Maybe you always go to sleep before your partner does in order to avoid sex, or maybe you're reluctant to even hold hands and kiss for fear it will lead to more. Start to **D**e-couple: Physical intimacy doesn't have to be perceived as a threat or demand for sexual intimacy. Proactively **E**ngage with your partner in new ways: Maybe there are activities, both sexual and non-sexual, that will make you start to feel more intimately connected. **R**egulate: When you feel a sense of panic or anxiety, when it feels as if your partner is pressuring you or not understanding you, don't let those feelings escalate and hijack you. Let your partner know what you're feeling as well as what you were trying to accomplish through the detox process.

KEEP IN MIND THE VALUE OF A FIVE TO ONE RATIO OF POSITIVE STATEMENTS.
Eminent marriage therapist John Gottman has spent a lifetime working with married couples, researching what makes some marriages succeed and others fail. Gottman concluded, "It is the balance between positive and negative emotional interactions in a marriage that determines its well-being—whether the good moments of mutual pleasure, passion, humor, support, kindness, and generosity outweigh the bad moments of complaining, criticism, anger, disgust, contempt, defensiveness, and coldness." Those couples that succeed in their marriages enjoy an overriding proportion of positive over negative sentiment. But how do you ensure that? "All

couples, happy and unhappy, have conflict, but the ratio of positive to negative interactions during arguments is a critical factor," and Gottman proposed that this ratio should, ideally, be five to one. While it's impossible to go through life tallying positive versus negative interactions, I've found that it is possible to determine intuitively whether your relationship is generally in the positive, or tending more toward the negative.

TRY TO DO AT LEAST ONE NEW THING TOGETHER. Use this new sense of connection to establish the foundation for a process of relationship renewal. As we discussed earlier, dopamine activity plays a key role in desire, but it also enables us to idealize the qualities in our partner we find most appealing. At the start of a relationship, dopamine activity enables us to see our mate with a "rose-colored tint" that filters out the negative. (How often do those quirky habits and eccentricities that we first adored in our partner eventually become the very things that annoy us?) By reinvesting our relationship with a sense of newness, however, we trigger that dopamine rush that allows us to surf on a hormonal wave of good feeling. And finding ways to remain focused on the positive without getting too bent out of shape about those irritating little things we once adored is critical to getting into the positive "five to one zone."

SENSATE FOCUS AND YOUR REJUVENATED SEX LIFE

To return to the earlier analogy of diagnosing an allergic reaction, we're going to perform a "relationship scratch test" of individual sexual interactions.

To do this, we will turn to the work of sex researchers William Masters and Virginia Johnson on "sensate focus," which utilizes a series of exercises that emphasize the focus on physical sensations. In traditional sensate focus, sex is taken off the table, and then gradually reintroduced, one aspect at time, which, from our perspective, makes it a natural extension of the Detox. Sensate focus takes couples through a process of touching, connection, and awareness, during which each partner takes turns as giver and receiver. The object of this is to develop a heightened sense of sexual self-awareness and a keener understanding of what feels good to their partner.

By removing the goal of intercourse during sensate focus, the couple is given the freedom to focus on sensual experiences that may have been ignored, missed, or glossed over in the goal-oriented rush toward sex and orgasm. Sensate focus takes the spotlight off of genital stimulation and enables individuals to experience pleasure throughout their entire bodies. It expands the erogenous landscape, and is a simple but powerful way to re-discover and touch anew. Like massage, sensate focus uses a targeted approach to uncover sexual pressure points and to address tension spots as they arise, and then work through them. Sensate focus hence reinforces the links between body and mind and enables us to connect more fully with our partner through sensual and sexual touch.

How and why does sensate focus accomplish a version of a relationship scratch test? One of the reasons is that sensual touch stimulates our natural cuddle chemicals, oxytocin in women and vasopressin in men, which induce a sense of attachment and emotional intimacy. Women generally produce more oxytocin than men, but men also produce high levels of oxytocin during sexual arousal and orgasm.

According to the *New Scientist* ("What Is This Thing Called Love?" April 29, 2006), "Oxytocin also boosts trust, which is an important step in developing a loving relationship." British scientist Andreas Meyer-Lindenberg and his team at the National Institute of Mental Health found that oxytocin release in research subjects "reduced activity in the amygdala, a part of the brain that signals fear, and therefore helped them to bond to another person." *So not only is sensual touch a path to rebuilding trust, via the release of oxytocin, but touch can also inform when there's an absence of trust, or a disconnection between mind and body, resulting in fear and insecurity.*

"In both males and females, oxytocin causes relaxation, fearlessness, bonding, and contentment with each other. And to maintain its effect long-term, the brain's attachment system needs repeated, almost daily activation through oxytocin stimulated by closeness and touch," writes Dr. Louann Brizendine, M.D., in her book *The Female Brain.* "Activities such as caressing, kissing, gazing, hugging and orgasm can replenish the chemical bond of love and trust." So as we move into the second stage of the Rejuvenation, as much as possible I would like you to complement all of your talks with your partner with the addition of hand-holding, hugging, and kissing (and lots of it). This will get the oxytocin flowing and facilitate a greater sense of intimacy. All it takes is a twenty-second hug to get the oxytocin flowing in women, but men need to be hugged three times as much as women to get to similar levels. So start hugging. If, as in many relationships, you and your partner have become physically disconnected, use this as your opportunity to start getting back "in touch" with each other.

STAGE 2: TOUCHING TO TUNE IN

Sensate focus is, as the name implies, a very sensual, hands-on approach to rebuilding sexual and emotional intimacy. In Stage 2, the couple takes turns giving and receiving, touching and being touched, but major erogenous zones (namely breasts and genitals) are strictly off limits. Our object is to develop a basic sense of touch while working through relationship obstacles that impede a sense of connection.

As an example, Emily was raised in a crowded home with brothers and sisters where privacy was at a premium and sex was never openly discussed. As a result she never got to know her own body and did not begin to masturbate until late into college. Until recently she was uncomfortable with masturbation and was inhibited about communicating her desires to sexual partners. To compensate, she had become a voracious and enthusiastic giver, and used porn to learn how to be sexy and turn on a man.

With a reputation for being sexual and "wild in bed," only she was aware of the irony that she was able to give but not receive and was the consummate faker. However, when Emily met and fell in love with Todd, she decided it was time to undertake the program. Throughout the Sex Detox, she unraveled the compound effects of how her early upbringing, parochial school education, and sexual indoctrination via mainstream media and porn had negatively affected her experience and enjoyment of sex. But it was the sensate focus exercises that finally allowed her to develop a constructive new roadmap to her own body. Through engaging in all four stages of the Rejuvenation with Todd, starting with basic touch, Emily was able to work through her inhibitions and all the memories and associations that informed them and develop a new unprecedented level of sexual and emotional intimacy.

It is important to note that during Stage 2 of the Rejuvenation, you will be touching simply to touch, without the express intention of eliciting arousal. While much of sensate focus ostensibly takes place on the surface of the body, what makes it so uniquely powerful is the mental/

emotional component. The internal work you did during the detox will begin to pay off during sensate focus. You will communicate, repair, test, and reinforce the new behavioral patterns and emotional underpinnings through the Stage 2 touching exercises.

Focus on caressing, which is not the same as giving a massage. Caressing is a lighter activity that is designed to awaken nerve endings. Switch off between giving and receiving with your partner. Focus on face, hands, and feet. Add kissing, but don't do these exercises to turn each other on; do them, rather, to comfort and connect with one another.

Some Techniques for Better Touching

In her book *Love Skills,* sex therapist Linda Devillers, Ph.D., describes a few types of touch that are best for these Stage 2 sensate focus exercises. They include:

- **FAN STROKES**—"With your hands side by side, keep your fingers close together, pointed in the direction you intend to stroke. Glide your hands over your lover's body, distributing light pressure evenly. As you caress, keep spreading your hands outward fluidly in opposite directions in the shape of a fan."

- **CIRCULAR STROKES**—"These feel particularly good on the back, thighs, and along the sides of the body. Use one or both hands to produce continuous, rounded strokes."

- **RAKING STROKES**—"Bend your fingers slightly so you're only using your fingertips. Or, if the receiver prefers, your fingernails. Begin with short strokes. Use both hands side-by-side or let them work independently. Create variety, suspense, and anticipation by raking at different speeds."

- **FEATHER STROKES**—"Possibly the most sensuous of all strokes. Imagine your fingertips as feathers. Let them glide over your lover's body, one hand following the other. Vary the speed and pressure— lingering at times, barely touching the surface at others."

As an example of some of the issues (as well as some of the revelations) that may arise during Stage 2 of the Rejuvenation, let's look at a patient of mine named Lauren, who undertook the program because she felt her fiancé, David, was taking her for granted, both in and out of the bedroom. Both of them had stressful jobs, but Lauren *alone* found herself doing a second shift when she got home: From shopping to cooking to cleaning, she was doing all the household work. Meanwhile David, who'd been raised in a traditional home, seemed to *expect* Lauren to do this, as he happily watched TV or caught up on his fantasy baseball games.

For Lauren, sex had become yet another chore, and another way in which David took her for granted. And, as with any chore, sex had grown routine and joyless. Worse, it had become a source of resentment. Lauren tried to talk with David about pitching in more around the apartment, and though he nodded as if he heard the words, his actions didn't change.

When Lauren told David she was going to undertake this Sex Detox, he instantly assumed she was withholding sex as a means of retaliation, the way his father had warned him women were apt to do.

At first he was angry with Lauren, both for "holding out" sexually and for leaving him to cook and to clean up after himself while she was off working on her Detox Diary. During this time, however, he began to realize just how much Lauren had been doing for him. He loved Lauren for who she was, but despite this realization, a part of him couldn't help wanting her to be more like his mother. He was happy to reap the bounty of their dual-income lives, but he was also angry with her for demanding that he do an equitable share of the housework. He was engaging in a double standard without even realizing it.

David shared his thoughts and revelations with Lauren and did his best to support her throughout the Detox. He was especially concerned that sex had become another chore on her daily to-do list, a situation he wanted to reverse. Lauren felt encouraged by David's understanding, and together they moved into the Stage 2 rejuvenation exercises.

But Lauren quickly found herself irritated by David's touch. As part of her commitment to the philosophy underlying the program, she shared her reactions with David. Needless to say, he was perturbed by what he perceived as her "sexual baby steps," but agreed to do his equal share around the house, since he knew it was only fair. It took a little while for Lauren to believe the changes David was making were genuine and more than just a means to get her back in the mood, but they continued working through the Stage 2 giving and receiving until they developed a renewed sense of physical connection supported by honest communication.

Over a period of time, Lauren and David were able to joke about the former inequity of their relationship and that playfulness diffused a lot of lingering resentment and facilitated greater bonding during their touch-and-hugging sessions. The ability to laugh at themselves had now become a new part of their rejuvenated love life, allowing them to experiment in ways they had never tried before with a sense of fun rather than obligation.

It's important that you have a base of loving, trusting, respectful touch like Lauren and David had before moving on to Stage 3. You might make it through all of Stage 2 in a few days or less. If so, great. But it's also possible that you and your partner have barriers to this form of touch. If so, think about those barriers and use this time to work through them, together.

Jackie and Dennis, both in their mid-twenties, prided themselves on being sexual thrill-seekers. Hooking up quickly and moving in together, their freewheeling sexual attitudes were an integral part of their identity as a couple. With strong sexual appetites and an open attitude, they consistently upped the ante: From role playing to making sex tapes to orchestrating threesomes, they were constantly in search of *more, more, more.* But both Jackie and Dennis came to me feeling that though the sex was, indeed, "hot," something felt hollow. They felt disconnected emotionally and like they were not maturing either separately or together.

With many of their friends getting married and having kids, they wanted more from their relationship, not just sex. They wanted to learn how to find sexual stimulation from within and truly "strip down" to the core.

For Jackie and Dennis, Stage 2 of the sensate focus exercises seemed remarkably simple and silly at first, but learning to slow down was at the heart of developing new rhythms in their relationship, and letting sex feed and nurture as opposed to just stimulate. They had to let go of their go-go sexual exploits and take some time to enjoy the quieter moments alone.

STAGE 3: TOUCHING TO TURN ON

In **Stage 3** of the Rejuvenation, we expand touch to include the erogenous zones, but it still excludes intercourse or any form of direct genital touching that leads to orgasm. The third stage begins only when *both* partners feel they are ready and have worked through Stage 2, eliminating the psychic and emotional barriers to luxuriating in each other's touch.

During this stage, you will be touching with the intent to arouse, but not necessarily with the goal of orgasmic gratification. You are casting aside your sex-scripts and developing new paths to sexual stimulation, and the lack of obligation to gratify helps to eliminate performance anxieties and pressures, allowing both participants to enjoy the moment for what it is.

Go back to your Detox Diary and reflect on the positive highlights of your sex life, those moments when you were the most turned on. Discuss what you enjoyed and how you and your partner can take those experiences as the starting point for a lifelong journey of sexual adventure and fulfillment. As you talk about your formative firsts and what you liked and disliked, employ the massage and caressing techniques discussed in Stage 2.

Continue, in turns, as giver and receiver. This time add sexual touch, but without too much direct genital stimulation or intentional stimulation to orgasm. Of course, accidents happen; enjoy them when they do, but don't go out of your way to facilitate their inevitability. Think of this as a very prolonged tease. A bit of light touching near the genitals is good, but visualize yourself pleasuring your lover in waves that take you toward the genitals and then away.

If you're experiencing tension, does it happen when you are on the giving or receiving end, or both? I often find that it's harder for women to receive pleasure than it is to give it, for a variety of reasons: body image, fear that they're taking too long, fear that he's not enjoying himself, fear of letting go, and the loss of conscious control that's crucial to female orgasm. Many books and magazines supply an overabundance of tips and techniques for giving, but they don't talk about the importance of being able to receive pleasure.

If you're a guy, you might feel uncomfortable about being vulnerable to receiving physical tenderness in a way that is not specifically sexual. Sex is one of the only situations in which guys actually give themselves permission to touch and be touched, and even then we often remain plagued by a sense of guardedness. The truth is that men love non-genital-based touch, but we're inhibited, sometimes even guilty, when it comes to asking for physical comfort. This ambivalence often stems from a number of underlying causes: a male sense of ego to take the lead in sexual interactions, a discomfort with submitting to a woman and abdicating control, a sense of emasculation when not focusing on performance/penetration and embarrassment at wanting to be stroked, flattered, and doted on (desires typically considered feminine).

I know it probably sounds simplistic, but when we're having sex we're giving and receiving simultaneously, and very often one process or set of experiences overrides or cancels out the other. As an example, many women tell me that when they're focused on pleasing men, they usually don't orgasm, because they can't mentally let go. According to recent investigations in the area of brain science, this is scientifically supported:

Researchers in the Netherlands found that "the key to female arousal seems to be deep relaxation and a lack of anxiety." In a study in which the brains of men and women were scanned during the process of sexual response using a technique called positron emission tomography (PET), the results showed that the parts of the female brain responsible for processing fear, anxiety, and emotion reduce during sexual activity. And at peak, during orgasm, the female brain's emotion centers close down, producing an almost trance-like state. Says Dr. Gert Holstege, "What this means is that deactivation, letting go of all fear and anxiety, might be the most important thing, even necessary, to have an orgasm." So if you're a woman, getting turned on also means, ironically, letting yourself get turned off.

For men the process of sexual response is laden with nuanced sensations and arousal at every turn, and many guys approach orgasm the way a kid does a gourmet dinner—rushing through one spectacular course to the next in order to get to dessert. While women are well aware that sex is more than orgasms, for many men, sexual interaction and orgasm are synonymous. Sex equals orgasm, and vice versa. Game over. In order to gain an ability to appreciate the entire meal, you both need to relax, slow down, and let go.

As an example, let's take a look at a former patient of mine named Evan. An advertising executive in his mid-thirties, Evan came to me because he had suffered from rapid ejaculation his entire adult life. He had developed massive insecurities, feeling that he was unable to "perform" like a "real man." Moreover, he refused to discuss the issue with his live-in girlfriend, Betsy. The silence that pervaded their sex life became riddled with simmering anxiety. The Sex Detox allowed Evan to come to terms with his feelings and communicate with Betsy in an open and positive way.

Betsy had no idea that he was suffering so much internally, and had always thought Evan was simply sexually selfish and short-sighted and incapable of physical affection. As a result, she had built up a lot of anger at his wham-bam-thank-you-ma'am approach to "lovemaking." Stage 3 of the Rejuvenation enabled Evan to realize just how much pleasure he could offer his girlfriend solely by being more sensual, playful, and communicative. During Stage 3, without the pressure to give Betsy an orgasm, Evan learned to give pleasure in ways other than uncontrollable penile thrusting: by learning to build arousal through prolonged teasing, intimate talking, and non-genital stroking. By the time they reached Stage 3, Betsy had worked up quite an appetite and was much more easily orgasmic. This allowed Evan to kick back and enjoy his orgasm without guilt or shame for the first time in his life.

STAGE 4: TOUCHING TO TRANSCEND

In the fourth and final stage of sensate focus, you are mutually touching and having orgasms (through any and all means possible that are mutually desirable). This is sex, but not as you've ever done it before. The key is that there are no established sex scripts and sex is an unpredictable journey, not as an isolated component of your life. This kind of sex is woven into the fabric of everything you do. As you learn to touch anew you will realize that much of that newness comes from not just how we touch each other physically, *but how well we stimulate each other's minds.*

Think about your foremost erotic fantasies, the ones that have returned time and again over the years, the ones that you wrote about during your Sex Detox. Share them with your partner.

Explore the Four Poles

The Four Poles that I am referring to are domination, submission, exhibitionism, and voyeurism, which we discussed during your Detox (see page 98). I want you and your partner to talk about these poles, and to discuss your feelings (and fantasies) about each one. Figure out where your common ground lies. Is light bondage your thing? Maybe the idea of having sex outside turns you on? Maybe a little playful exhibitionism— being sexual in public or semi-public, where there's a risk of being caught or observed—is the jolt of sexual adrenaline you need to boost those dopamine levels to new highs. (Not to be confused with public sex, which could get you arrested or seriously embarrassed, playful exhibitionism is about making the most of quick moments to stimulate the mind and get the heart pounding.) It's important to understand that what matters most is not covering the bases of kinky sex. It's about exploring your unique love maps together, ultimately creating a common love map. It's about bringing your intellect, your emotions, your past, and your future into the current moment in a vital and exciting way.

Good sex is not a recipe book of positions or naughty fetishes you find on a web site. It's talking and tuning in. It's understanding each other inside and out: physically, emotionally, and sexually. It's about being in the moment in a fully embodied (and very present) way. If you want to try tying each other up, go for it. If you want to get a video camera or simply plan what you would do if you were going to film yourselves, that's great. *But,* you shouldn't confuse those acts with "hot sex." Because what you have hopefully learned throughout the Sex Detox, and beyond, is that what turns you on is different than what turns your partner (and everyone else) on. What matters is learning how to talk about what you like and don't like together, whether it's a particular position or an elaborate fantasy. It's about achieving a new level of absolute trust and intimacy that allows you to explore pleasure in all its dimensions.

For example, Michelle came to me complaining of low desire, debilitating sexual inhibitions, and a chronic tendency to fake orgasms with Hank, her husband of many years.

One issue that came up time and again regarding her sense of "sexual disconnection" with her husband was his desire to have a threesome. She was insulted that he wanted to bring another woman into the bedroom, and felt his fantasy indicated a basic lack of maturity and an insensitivity to her desires. For his part, Hank felt as if he'd married a prude, and was becoming increasingly convinced that they were sexually incompatible. It wasn't just about the threesome, but how routine their sex life had become. Meanwhile, Michelle worried what *else* he wanted to do and was concerned about opening a door that she might not be able to shut. Nonetheless, she hated being cast as a prude: In truth, she had an extremely vivid fantasy life and had been somewhat adventurous in her early twenties. In fact, she had participated in a threesome in graduate school. She had been extremely turned on by the idea at the time, until it actually happened and her boyfriend wound up dumping her for the other woman.

Now, years later, whenever Hank mentioned a threesome, she couldn't help but recall the negative emotions that had come up as a result of her previous experience and reacted to her husband with an anger that drew its force from the past. Until the Detox, she had not dealt with these feelings, nor had she shared her past experience with her husband, for fear he would view her as a hypocrite.

But once the lines of communication were open and she had fully disclosed her past, Hank did not respond the way Michelle expected. Instead of pressuring her into a repeat performance with him, he was sympathetic and said that not only did he not want to push her into having a threesome, but he wanted to support her in any way possible. His sense of understanding and empathy was surprising to Michelle, and it inspired in her a wish to be more sexually adventurous. She wasn't sure if she would ever want to have a threesome, but that didn't mean she wouldn't fantasize and role play with Hank about it, knowing now that he would never push her to do something she didn't want to do.

During Stage 4 of the Rejuvenation, Michelle found that she enjoyed fantasizing with Hank about having a threesome, which included commenting on the sexiness of other women they saw out and about in public. This fueled their imaginations and desire, and made their interaction in the bedroom all the hotter. As happens with many couples, the disparate and disconnected sexual fantasies that had initially played a divisive role in their relationship now united them and ushered them into an exciting world of shared sexual fantasies and sensual and erotic pleasure. And like so many, once she opened the lines of sexual communication with her husband, she found it was easy, fun, and rejuvenating to keep them open.

BEYOND THE BIG BANG

John and Paula came to me seven years into their relationship, having met when they were both seniors in college. During the first six months of dating, the sex was hot and frequent, though not wildly experimental. They moved in together shortly thereafter, mostly owing to the economics of maintaining separate residences in Manhattan. During this time, the sex quickly ebbed to warm and affectionate lovemaking once or twice a week with no frills attached. By the time they were married a few years later, their sex life had waned to a take-it-or-leave-it once-a-month schedule. Realizing they had to fix things before they complicated matters by starting a family, they came to see me.

During the Detox part of the program, which Paula undertook on her own (but which John fully supported), she went back and retraced some of her issues to her parents' relationship. Amicable, but never physically affectionate with each other, her parents could openly discuss the birds and the bees, but it never seemed to her that they were utilizing these skills, so to speak. Much like her mother, Paula was a chronic dieter and had low self-esteem with regard to her body image, such that she felt very uncomfortable nude. Exacerbated by the images she saw in popular culture, this insecurity negatively affected her formative firsts. She felt unsexy and unattractive and only was willing to "do it with the lights off."

Her sexual experiences prior to meeting John were few and far between: a couple of drunken encounters during parties that ended in unsatisfying fumblings, followed by a brief relationship in her first year of college during which she lost her virginity. Soon after, the guy left her for someone "hotter." She had a couple of isolated one- or two-night stands and then she met John. They started out as study partners and became friends. She helped him through the end of a bad relationship and grew to trust him enough to believe he cared about her with all his heart.

As a result, she was able to have sex like never before. Not exactly with the lights on, but it was satisfying for both of them.

Paula never worked through her issues, however. So once the rush of infatuation dampened, her earlier hang-ups resurfaced. By retracing early associations and memories that fed into her love map during the initial Sex Detox, she was ready, willing, and able by the start of the Rejuvenation to begin rewiring herself to explore sex in a more fully embodied way. She discussed the issues with John during Stage 2 of the Rejuvenation, accompanied by lots of sensate touching and cuddling that helped strengthen their emotional bond and promote trust and comfort.

During the second stage, they worked on revisiting the good and bad parts of Paula's past sexual experiences—the excitement of making out for the first time, her early erotic fantasies and memories, together with non-intercourse-driven touch and play, which allowed her to bask in being turned on and connected without the "punch line" of orgasmic release.

By Stage 3, Paula was ready to put it all together, and the couple spent two straight days and nights touching and caressing and fondling each other while sharing their secret fantasies. They did not have a lot of intercourse during this time, but rather luxuriated in taking and being taken, in giving and receiving pleasure, and engaging each other mentally.

Six months later, Paula came in for a follow-up and told me the sex was better than ever. It was "qualitatively different," as she put it, more patient, more tender, more connected. They always talked during sex these days, which turned them both on, coming up with new fantasies together. As a result of the Detox, Paula went from being lights off to having all the bulbs turned on and burning brightly.

And while they had incorporated intercourse back into their sexual activities more often, they had not lost sight of the core significance of giving and receiving pleasure. Their lovemaking was no longer an eight-minute trip to obligation and back. It was a source of emotional sustenance and comfort laced with sensual pleasure and lusty desire.

What it all comes down to as this program ends and your lifelong sexual journey continues is the need to open yourself up to your partner and to learn to experience sexual and sensual pleasure with every ounce of your being. Embrace the wondrous landscape of your unique memories, associations, fantasies, and formative experiences with eyes wide open and fully fixed on each other. Regardless of what forms your desires take and where your new love maps may lead, what makes sex truly sexy is not a particular fetish, position, or disproportionately large body part, it's sharing every breathtaking secret and sensation with someone you love.

You only have one love life. Live it to the fullest.

Your *Sex Detox* experience continues at www.IanKerner.com, where you will find additional content, a community, and a growing directory of resources to supplement your journey to relationship renewal.

PART III

The Singles' Detox

8.

Background to the Singles' Detox

As we discussed in Part I, just as a physical fast will alter your metabolism and natural body chemistry, this program is going to affect (and, in some ways, "alter") your neurochemistry, enabling you to reset, rewire, and, ultimately, rejuvenate your love life. So if you're restlessly single in search of a lasting connection, you need to liberate yourself from those negative patterns (which are now part of your "dating DNA") and find a healthier way of dating and relating. That means for the next thirty days, no dating and no seeking out dates or putting yourself in situations (whether online in the virtual world or offline in the real world) that are either directly or indirectly about dating. If you're getting over a breakup and still thinking about your ex, it's time to go cold turkey. This is your chance to cleanse and renew and give yourself a fresh start. By retracing the roots of your goals, desires, and dating habits, we will replace negative patterns with healthy ones that align more fully with your long-term needs. And this in turn will not just give you a better psychological framework for understanding how you date and relate, but will ultimately enable you to take clearer, more successful steps in living your love life to the fullest.

ADDING A SEX FAST TO YOUR DETOX

In the service of the broader principle of "out with the old in with the new," your Dating Detox will include a sex fast as well. In today's world, casual sex is as common as fast-food. And the long-term effects can be just as pernicious: Hopeful hook-ups dull your appetite for intimacy while feeding you non-satisfying dribs and drabs of temporary fulfillment.

As I've often remarked, just because we treat sex lightly doesn't mean sex will treat us lightly in return. Too often, casual sex is a potent reminder of the relationship we're not having, the intimacy we would like to be having, and the fact that we're merely having sex when what we really want is to be in love.

Such was certainly the case for a patient of mine, Lola, who described herself as a "binge-and-purge dater" during our initial exploratory session. She was, at the time, a twenty-eight-year-old marketing manager for a high-end shoe designer. She lived in New York City with two roommates, one cat, and no "serious" boyfriend. Her last serious relationship of three years ended shortly after college graduation, when her boyfriend decided he wanted to "find himself" on the West Coast, where he remains to this day. Lola led an active social life and went out quite often, including regular sojourns to clubs and parties where she sometimes hooked up with men on the first or second date in the hope that it might evolve into "something real." But none of these liaisons had in fact resulted in more than three- or four-month sex-based flings, which usually frittered away to nothingness just as quickly as they began, leaving her feeling depressed and insecure. For Lola, sex had become a stopgap, a way of avoiding loneliness in the short-term, but at the expense of long-term happiness and fulfillment.

Tired of the yo-yo dating cycle from hopeful hook *up* to dejected let *down*, Lola turned to counseling and was able to cleanse her sexual palate and boost her self-confidence through a carefully staged program of sexual fasting and dating detoxification. And if Lola can rejuvenate, ready herself, and ultimately find love as a result of this program, so can you.

9.

The Singles' Detox

Over the next thirty days, you will be immersed in what I hope is a life-altering experience: the detox phase of this program. If you follow this step-by-step plan, broken up into six five-day modules, and commit yourself to both the Detox and the rejuvenation phase that follows, you will drastically improve your self-awareness, self-esteem, and ability to achieve long-term fulfillment. This is not a miracle plan or a magic act. What you get out of the program will depend directly on how focused you are and how much work you put into it.

You'll probably find that some areas of your sex and/or dating life are more toxic than others, while perhaps some areas are quite healthy. Our goal over the next thirty days is to swing the pendulum from toxicity to health in all areas of your love life.

In addition to an initial detox diagnostic, each module contains *Detox Diary assignments* (these typically call for self-reflection) as well as *engagement exercises* that will help crystallize the work you're doing.

In terms of the overall duration of the Detox, thirty days is not an arbitrary number. In my work with patients, a month turns out to be just about the perfect amount of time to work through the modules, to rise above the issues, and to purge the toxicity. That said, you should feel comfortable working at your own pace. If you finish a module in less than five days, feel free to move on. On the other hand, if you find yourself needing more time, then by all means, take it. But try as much as possible to undertake the detox sequence continuously, without interruption, in order to maintain a steady sense of deepening self-reflection.

Please know that even though you are doing this on your own, *you are not going it alone.* The experience continues at www.IanKerner.com.

MODULE 1: STARTING UP
Days 1 to 5

Day 1

PREPARE

Find a private moment where you can take up to a half hour to yourself. Trust me, I know it's not easy: For many of you, finding this small window of time may be the most challenging thing I ask. Ideally it will occur during a time of day and in a physical place where you will be uninterrupted. If possible, dedicate a quiet place in your home to the Detox and return to this same place every day at the same time, as this consistency will give you a sense of comfort and routine, and this place may even prove to be a source of refuge long after the Detox is over. (Don't worry if that quiet place ends up being a bathroom, rooftop, or even a closet—one guy I worked with ended up sitting in the stairwell of his apartment building.)

Whether you're more comfortable with a notebook and pen or your laptop, you should set up a Detox Diary. In it you will record your thoughts, emotions, and observations. Keep your Detox Diary in a shoebox (or something similar), which you can also use as a place to store or memorialize letters, photos, and other symbolic images or actual mementos from your past. This is more than mere journal keeping. This diary will be a living totem of your Detox and a way to visualize your journey.

BREATHE

Before you begin the start-up diagnostic, spend up to five minutes relaxing and breathing. Throughout the Detox you will use breathing to calm yourself and to transition from the outside world into this new private interior space of meditation and reflection.

- **YOUR THOUGHTS.** As you do this, try to empty yourself of thoughts and turn off any internal monologues. If you find yourself having trouble, do your best to hone in on the recurring messages and themes so you can record them when you're done, as they will serve as a window into your core anxieties and help you to take a positive step toward enhanced self-awareness.

- **YOUR FEELINGS.** Focus on the feelings that accompany this five-minute meditation cycle. Does the sense of calm and interior reflection incite guilt or panic? Anxiety and restlessness? Arousal or exhaustion? Boredom? You'll record your feelings in your diary and keep a close eye on how they evolve throughout the entirety of this program.

Each day when you have finished your breathing exercises, open your journal and start off by recording your "breathing thoughts and feelings." Take a moment to consider—are there any natural connections between your breathing thoughts and emotions?

As an example, one single I guy worked with, Lloyd, couldn't stop thinking about all the people who might be trying to reach him via his cell phone and BlackBerry (for Lloyd, his BlackBerry really had become his "crackberry") during this period of reflection. Even though he had created a private space for himself, he still felt surrounded by a swirl of information and couldn't calm down: his breathing emotions were anxiety and a sense of dread, while his breathing thoughts were "missing important calls and messages" and "not being able to be reached." At first Lloyd thought this was a natural work-related panic, but upon further reflection, he began to see how truly afraid he was of being alone. Like many, he had been using the gadgets of our inter-connected age to mask and block out his panic at being disconnected. For Lloyd, just being able to take a fraction of an hour for himself was a powerful, if frightening, first step.

So think about the connection between your breathing thoughts and breathing emotions, and take a few minutes to write down any connections, both obvious and perhaps far-fetched. Then dig a little deeper. Like Lloyd, is there a hidden anxiety lurking just below the surface with you as well? Give yourself a chance to speculate. You won't know for sure if you don't allow yourself to ruminate.

THE DETOX DIAGNOSTIC

Take as much time as you need to answer the following questions. If a particular question is not applicable, don't answer it. If there doesn't seem to be an appropriate answer, then pick the one that's closest, but in your Detox Diary, write the response that would be more appropriate. If any other thoughts come to mind while you're answering a question, write them down. (Don't worry about your responses—the questionnaire is not intended to be a clinical evaluation but rather a catalyst for contemplating the issues and generally getting the ball rolling.)

How Toxic Is Your Dating/Sex Life?

1. I most often meet the people I date:

   a. Through a variety of means, including: friends and setups, being out and about, and via the Internet, school, work, or some form of shared community.

   b. Through just one outlet.

   c. Almost never. I've stopped actively trying to date.

2. As a whole, my dating life has been:

   a. Really satisfying.

   b. Sometimes satisfying.

   c. Rarely to never satisfying.

3. When I go out on dates, I:

   a. Don't expect anything serious to come of it, but am eager to be happily surprised.

   b. Hope my date and I will instantly click and that he or she may be "the one," although I try to be somewhat open-minded.

   c. I generally determine if they fit my list of dating criteria by the time I'm ready to bail on dessert.

4. When a first date doesn't go well and he or she doesn't call me (back) for a second date, I:

   a. Realize it probably wasn't meant to be and move on.

   b. Feel a sting of rejection and worry that I'm not projecting the qualities that will win me a mate.

   c. Take it as a sign that I don't cut it in the dating scene and that I'm just not attractive and successful enough to find a partner.

5. In terms of dating frequency, I would say that I:

   a. Go on exactly the number of dates I want to, which is more or less depending on other stuff going on in my life with work, hobbies, and friends.

   b. Go on more dates than I want with folks I don't even like, because I'm terrified of missing out on landing a semi-decent partner.

   c. Go on very few dates, because there's no use going through the trouble of making an effort just to be disappointed and rejected again.

6. Which of the following sets of terms most accurately describes your feelings toward dating (while some of the adjectives may not fit, pick the category that comes closest to matching your current emotional state):

   a. Fun, exciting, optimistic, energizing, engaging, exhilarating, sexy, imaginative, comforting, relaxing, flirtatious, empowering, naughty, titillating.

   b. Tedious, stressful, aggravating, frustrating, disappointing, annoying, upsetting, exasperating, addictive.

   c. Detached, boring, indifferent, pointless, empty, vapid, uninspiring, same ol' same ol', predictable.

7. When I think back on my early dating experiences, it makes me:

   a. Somewhat nostalgic for the carefree days when all I thought about was having fun.

   b. Wish I had enjoyed it more while I had the chance.

   c. Panicked that I missed the boat on finding a great partner and now everyone good is taken.

8. In past relationships, sex was:

   a. Fun and exciting in different ways with different people, depending on our particular chemistry.

   b. Somewhat disappointing, although I wasn't comfortable talking about it or working on it.

   c. Always a disappointment.

9. Over the course of my past dating and relationship experiences, I feel I have:

   a. Evolved and have gotten to know who I am and what I want/need.

   b. Grown, but feel a little bruised and worn for the wear.

   c. Been damaged and depleted of the core facility for personal growth and emotional trust.

10. In reviewing my past relationships I would say that they ended:

   a. Because I realized the person would never be a good partner for me over the long haul.

   b. Because I stopped trying and/or they stopped calling.

   c. Due to irrational or sabotaging behavior on my part, such as jealousy or commitment phobia.

11. When I look back on my serious relationships, I feel:

   a. Fondness but no sense of loss or regret.

   b. Regret for a certain lost love(s).

   c. Despair that I have not and may never meet "the one."

12. My estimation of the available singles pool is:

   a. There are a lot of great people out there, and if I spend enough time looking, I'll meet someone who's right for me.

b. Most of the good ones are taken, but it's not entirely hopeless.

c. I don't know why I even bother, the only folks who are still single are either not capable of a serious relationship, second-hand goods, or total wack jobs.

13. With regard to finding a partner, I believe:

a. There is no such thing as "the one," but rather a number of people with whom I could share enough of the same interests and values to build a happy and meaningful relationship.

b. There are probably only one or two people with whom I would be ideally matched, but given the realities of biology and timing, I'm willing to settle for a close second.

c. There is only one soul mate per customer, and either you wind up meeting or you wind up alone.

14. In terms of a potential partner, I believe:

a. Everybody has strengths and weaknesses, and it's a question of finding someone whose good qualities outweigh their bad, based on mutual interests and desires.

b. It's important to work through all areas of incompatibility before committing.

c. It doesn't matter what they're like; if they have any baseline potential whatsoever, I will mold them into who I want them to be!

15. For me, dating is a way to:

a. Meet people with whom I share enough in common to have a good time and possibly build a friendship or more.

b. Check out as many people as possible, hoping maybe one of them will work out as a partner (hey, I'm running out of time here)!

c. Keep myself from committing suicide or getting clinically obese.

16. When I am not seriously dating someone:

a. I make regular plans with friends or family and have a good time.

b. I make tentative plans with friends or family, but drop them cold if something better comes along (that is, a date).

c. I sit at home and check my email and usually get depressed or overeat.

17. In terms of when I choose to have sex in the early stages of dating, I usually:

a. Wait until I feel like it's the right time to be intimate, regardless of whether it's a first date or tenth.

b. Always wait until the third date, so I don't seem too easy or uptight.

c. Even though I usually regret it, I just can't bring myself to say no.

18. In terms of my overall body image, I am:

a. Pretty darn happy with how I look and feel, in clothes and out.

b. Generally comfortable, but somewhat insecure about having a little too much here and not enough there.

c. Self-conscious and uncomfortable.

19. When it comes to dating and sex:

a. I feel like I have a good basic awareness of what I want and need and how to get it.

b. I sometimes find myself in relationships based on guilt or lack of anything better on the immediate horizon.

c. Usually settle for whatever comes my way and deal with the consequences of getting out later.

20. When it comes to telling a partner what I want and need in bed, I am:

a. Very forthcoming—after all, it's in both of our best interests.

b. Fairly communicative, provided it doesn't make me seem unsexy or difficult to please.

c. I don't feel comfortable or even know for sure what I want in bed.

21. If I met someone I felt a serious connection with whom I wanted to be monogamous, I would:

a. Focus on seeing where the relationship went and stop shopping around.

b. Focus on the relationship, but still keep my eyes open just in case it doesn't work out.

c. Secretly date other people, since I don't want to lose out on any better options that come along or get tied down until it's a done deal.

22. My parents*:

a. Had a loving relationship that included a lot of affection and displays of love.

b. Were primarily friends and not terribly affectionate.

c. Were not loving or friendly to each other.

23. My parents were:

a. Open to talking about sex, love, and that kind of thing.

b. Not especially open, but did their best to answer my questions.

c. Not open to talking about sex.

24. With regard to my dating and sexual activities, my parents:

a. Were supportive of my sexuality and my early romantic interests.

b. Took a "don't ask, don't tell" approach.

c. Were absent or outright unsupportive of my sexuality and romantic interests.

25. I was raised in an environment in which sexuality was:

a. Treated as a normal, healthy, and natural development.

b. Quietly accepted but not openly discussed.

c. Shrouded in silence and/or shame.

26. My first exposures to sexuality came from:

a. Discussions with my parents supplemented by information at school from teachers and peers.

---

* Please note that when I ask you to think about your parents, I'm referring to the adults who raised you, regardless of whether or not one or both were your birth parents.

   b. Sex education at school, supplemented only by what I could pick up from siblings and peers.

   c. Wherever I could sniff it out, say dirty movies and magazines and eavesdropping.

It's time to score your answers:

FOR EVERY A, give yourself 3 points.

FOR EVERY B, give yourself 2 points.

FOR EVERY C, give yourself 1 point.

If you scored 50 points or more, you are more than likely still hopeful and optimistic and definitely primed for positive change and emotional and sexual intimacy. Your upbringing is unlikely to impede your ability to have a healthy sex life.

If you scored between 38 and 49 points, you are probably a little worn for the emotional wear, but you have plenty of good energy left to commit to change and positive growth. You will have to work on overcoming some of the negative patterns in your past that have marred your sexual self-esteem, but you have the underlying desire and ability to make your love life work.

If you scored under 38 points, then it may be a bumpy ride toward positive growth. You've likely run yourself ragged emotionally and sexually and come out feeling depleted. You are going to have to work on rebuilding your sexual self-esteem and work on developing healthier patterns of behavior. If you're getting over a breakup, how do you think your ex would have responded to the dating diagnostic? Do you recognize some fundamental areas of difference?

Take a few deep breaths and decompress. And congratulate yourself on taking the first step toward changing your love life.

See you tomorrow.

Day 2

Per Day 1, begin with the breathing exercise. We are going to start each day with this exercise (see page 142 for a reminder). Remember to jot down your "breathing thoughts" and "breathing emotions."

Today's main activity is going to involve working in your Detox Diary:

• Take a few minutes to look over the detox diagnostic that you completed yesterday. Would you answer the same way? In retrospect, do you believe you were as honest as possible? Do you see any new connections?

• Jot down the terms listed below.

My parents' relationship(s)
My early (mis)conceptions of sexuality
My first forays into sexual activity
My self-esteem
My current dating habits
My previous relationships
My long-term relationship goals

Now connect the terms. By this I mean, start with one term, and think about the connection to another term and keep it going until you've touched on all of the terms, or as many as seem relevant.

As an example, let's take a look at how this same exercise was completed by a former patient of mine named Tara, a single thirty-three-year-old real estate broker who currently lives in her hometown of Columbus, Ohio:

• **MY PARENTS' RELATIONSHIP** is connected to **MY LONG-TERM RELA-TIONSHIP GOALS** in that their relationship was always an inspiration and set the basic standard for what I eventually wanted. At the same time, I wouldn't want such a traditional relationship. My mother never worked outside the home, and I'd like a husband who's somewhat more "present" and more hands-on than my dad was during my childhood. I guess their relationship set up an idealistic yet unattainable goal.

- **MY LONG-TERM RELATIONSHIP GOALS** are connected to my **SELF-ESTEEM** in that I feel really bad that I'm not married yet. I never thought that I would be single at my age. I see all my old friends with husbands and kids, and I start to feel like there must be something seriously wrong with me. I just don't understand why nobody has chosen me by now.

- **MY SELF-ESTEEM** is related to my **CURRENT DATING HABITS.** I feel like I'm losing time. Nobody wants to start a family with a woman in her mid-thirties. So I keep on going out with these guys I honestly don't like, figuring maybe I can fix them or work with them, but then they just don't measure up and I'm back in the same sinking boat all over again.

- **MY CURRENT DATING HABITS** are connected to my **EARLY MISCONCEPTIONS OF SEXUALITY** in that I don't believe in making it easy for a guy sexually, regardless of what I may desire for myself. My mother waited until she and my dad were engaged, and they've always told me that if a guy really likes you, he'll be willing to wait for it. But by the time I usually wind up having sex with a guy, he's already lost interest. All I know is all the slutty girls from high school and college are already married, while here I am with my stupid high standards sleeping alone!

- **MY EARLY MISCONCEPTIONS OF SEXUALITY** are connected to my **FIRST FORAYS INTO SEXUAL ACTIVITY** in that I went all the way with my boyfriend in high school before I was ready, thinking we were going to get married. Then he dumped me before we went to college, and I felt really used and humiliated. And I think it colored my ability to trust men and made me associate sex with rejection.

• **MY FIRST FORAYS INTO SEXUAL ACTIVITY** are connected to my **PREVI-OUS RELATIONSHIPS** in that after my first time I was very wary of trusting men when it came to sex. And I think instead of enjoying what we were doing, I was always injecting sex with too much suspicion and paranoid distrust to be able to enjoy it. So it wound up becoming a self-fulfilling prophecy, because soon after the relationship became sexual, the guy would be out the door.

Once you get going you'll find it's easy to make connections. And that's the point of this exercise: *realizing that our dating and sexual identities are more than a finite set of likes and dislikes, but are rather an interrelated set of experiences that have forged patterns that are hard to break.*

Reread "your story" at the end of the day. See if you come up with even more connections. You'll find that all the items link up to each other in new and surprising ways. All you have to do is connect the dots to see the patterns emerge. If you're getting over a breakup, review your story through the lens of that relationship and see if there are any new details to add. For example, Tara focused on how her anxiety and sense of insecurity led to feelings of irrational jealousy whenever her ex-boyfriend interacted with one of his many female friends. Now gather a few key photos or keepsakes or jot down some names and terms on separate scraps of paper (for instance, a prom photo, the name of the person you lost your virginity to, a ticket stub from your first date, or a downloaded image of a red Mustang convertible) and place them in your memory box. Think about how those items fit together and tell a story.

Then take a few deep breaths and decompress.

See you tomorrow.

Day 3

Begin with your breathing exercises.

Take a few moments to review your Detox Diary. Is there anything you'd like to add to any of the entries so far? When you read it over, how does it make you feel? Depressed or scared? Relieved, excited? Helpless? Hopeful? What are the emotions that each story and memory brings up in you?

Today you're going to be reviewing the assignment you did yesterday in order to begin the hard work of separating the positive influences from the negative ones that inform your current dating habits, shape your expectations, and impact your self-esteem.

In your Detox Diary, create two columns labeled "pros" and "cons." In the left margin you'll write down the terms we began to think about yesterday, leaving enough space between entries to fill things in as you go. Once you're done, write down all the phrases and words that immediately come to mind, allotting yourself roughly five minutes to complete each set. Don't overthink this or write out beautiful, carefully worded poetic stories of true love and heartache. On the contrary, I would just list the adjectives and associations that immediately come to mind without pausing to censor your thoughts at all. For example, here's how a patient of mine, Renee, filled out her list:

	Pros	Cons
PARENTS' RELATIONSHIP(S)	· Always seemed unified · Very supportive of each other	· Very traditional gender roles · Not physically affectionate
EARLY (MIS)CON- CEPTIONS OF SEXUALITY	· Thought sex/love were inherently linked · Believed my desirability stemmed from looking pretty and dressing well	· Thought sex/love were inherently linked · Thought men were to be reined in

(continued)

	Pros	**Cons**
SELF-ESTEEM	· Parents made me feel very special · I knew I was pretty at a very young age	· Mom said being pretty was the key to getting a husband · I didn't necessarily develop my "internal" characteristics as much, and am insecure about my intellect
CURRENT DATING HABITS	· I get asked out on plenty of dates · I am always up front about what I'm looking for	· Nobody has what I'm looking for · I tend to write guys off for very shallow mistakes
PREVIOUS RELATIONSHIPS	· The first several months are amazing	· After a while they stop trying and I feel insecure and hurt and break up
LONG-TERM RELATIONSHIP GOALS	· I want a husband who treats me with adulation and tenderness	· I think I have 1950s views of marriage

When you have brainstormed as many bullet points as possible under each category, try to recall a recent date you went on. How many of the issues that you identified extending back through childhood, both positive and negative, in some way(s) affected your enjoyment of the date?

Take a few deep breaths and decompress.

See you tomorrow.

Day 4

By now your breathing exercises should be emerging as a regular practice. As you enter Day 4 of the program, think about whether this part of your daily routine has become a source of stress or one of comfort, or one that you've been having difficulty making a habit of.

Today's main focus will be exploring how your "dating fantasies" stack up against reality. Now, we all have certain types we're attracted to, and much of this is defined by physical features. And that's okay. Life comes in enough flavors to suit all tastes. But often when someone is drawn to a particular type, they often choose partners on that basis alone without factoring in all the other dimensions of the person's character and interests. The result is that the person who may *look* like your ideal mate on the outside is actually wrong for you in a number of ways. In your Detox Diary:

1. Describe what you thought your life would look like right now when you were, say, ten years old. Where did you see yourself? Were you married? If so, to whom? Did you have children, a house?

2. Now, describe how your life actually looks. Compare the two versions you have written and note the differences in language and tone. Is your childhood vision of where you thought you'd be full of positive and rosy words? And is your current view possibly a bit too hard on yourself?

3. Now, think about the person who you feel is your "ideal" mate. Describe this person in your Detox Diary. Be as vivid and as descriptive as you would like. Note any detail that comes to mind.

4. Review your description. Is it mainly physical? Or did you spend more time talking about this person's values and their internal makeup?

5. When you think of your ideal person, how much of what you describe comes from images and ideas that you have seen "externally" (that is, from the media or other sources)? How much of it is based on past loves and crushes?

6. Now, think about all of the standards you are applying to this ideal person, and turn the lens toward yourself. Try to write about yourself through the eyes of another person describing their ideal. Do you think you measure up? Can you see how sometimes you (and the people you date) set impossibly high standards?

Think about how your views of yourself have evolved over the years regarding what you want and expect from yourself as an ideal mate. Perhaps when you were fresh out of college and not as heavily involved in your career, your idea of being someone's ideal mate was being impulsive and romantic, always dressed to tease and please, ready to go careening into the sunset.

Perhaps now, your idea has changed. Being someone's be-all and end-all might not seem quite as intoxicating. In fact, it may induce night-sweats. Perhaps you have had your share of clingy partners, and now you realize you don't want someone who would preempt your independent interests. Perhaps being hot for adventure has given way to being supportive of another person's aspirations. And maybe your idea of the perfect weeknight escapade involves a quiet dinner for two, not clubbing until all hours of the night. The questions remain: Are you looking for what you used to want in a partner or what you actually want today? Are you in tune with your present-day desires, or are you living in the past?

For example, when I was single in my late twenties, I would have probably described my ideal mate as spontaneous, wild, beautiful, free-spirited, untethered by mainstream ambitions and expectations, eager to please. Today, if I had to make the same list, I would say, smart, independent, fit, attractive, responsible, professionally driven, and passionate yet practical.

At the end of the day, I want you to reread what you wrote. Are the people you've been dating reflective of outgrown views of what you want and need in a partner? Are you finding that some of the old items on your wish list are not only not what you want, but causing you to choose the wrong kinds of dates again and again? Be honest, we've all been there.

Take a deep breath and decompress.

See you tomorrow.

Day 5

At the conclusion of every five-day module, it's time for some module ending or "ME" time. This is a gift you'll give yourself for undertaking the Detox and for reaching the end of a module. This can include anything from getting a massage to taking a walk in the park. The key thing is it has to be done alone. In addition, I ask that you abide by the following rules:

- Try to make it something you've never done before or haven't done in a while (for example a seaweed wrap, a bike ride to an unfamiliar place, or a trip to a museum you've never been to before).

- You have to leave the house to do it.

- Don't resort to retail therapy.

- You should do something that allows you to focus on your interior thoughts. Hence, a movie or a play would not work.

- Place a memento relating to your outing in your memory box.

You did it! You have now completed the first module of the Detox. In many ways, this is the hardest part—getting started.

I hope you've started to see just how multifaceted and interconnected your love life is; how much of what you experience to this day is rooted in feelings and experiences that occurred in the past. By now you should be recognizing various common themes or patterns that have emerged repeatedly in your relationships. But don't worry if it all still feels a bit unclear. You're on the road to rejuvenation, and that's the important part.

Take a few deep breaths and decompress.

See you tomorrow.

MODULE 2: YOUR DATING HEALTH AND OUTLOOK
Days 6 to 10

Now that you've explored the inter-connectedness of the various dimensions of your dating and sex life, it's time to spend time delving more deeply into each one. This module—*Your Dating Health and Outlook*—comes early in the detox calendar because I feel it is important that you gain awareness into some of the factors impacting your dating life that you might not normally think about, such as how much pressure you are putting on individual dates. The goal of this module is to determine your level of dating health and get you on the road to improvement with a "clean bill of dating health."

Day 6

Begin this day as always with your breathing exercises.

Today we will be considering how your previous dating experiences have shaped your attitudes and patterns of dating to this day:

What kind of dating vibes are you sending? Are you free and easy or a dating worrywart? If you're taking this detox program, chances are you're trying to improve certain aspects of your romantic life. And as you know from the initial module, there are a lot of different things that can contribute to your success in the dating world. One of the main aspects of your dating "health" is your outlook. Believe it or not, that outlook can actually shape the destiny of a date. Now, I'm not suggesting that you can control the future. But if you are the type who goes into a date always "worrying" whether this will be the one or not, you might be inadvertently transferring some of that negative energy into the date itself. This can affect the way you "look" on the date (your smile, your body language), the way you act, and the way you communicate. How healthy is your outlook?

Answer the following questions in your Detox Diary:

1. Do you get the pre-date jitters, worrying about every last detail?

2. Are you results driven or open to whatever the experience might yield?

3. Do you ever date just for the fun of it (meaning, not for any end goal)?

4. Do you get antsy after a date? Do you feel that you want to call or email that person right away to find out if they want to see you again?

5. Even if you don't click with a person, do you harbor feelings of wanting them to have liked you?

HOW SELF-AWARE ARE YOU?

"Know thyself," say the poets. And there is no better advice for those who are dating. If you don't know yourself, then how can you be in any position to determine what it is you want, and what type of person you want in your life? A lot of people think that having a very narrowly defined type means that they know themselves. But when one truly knows him or herself, one approaches the world with an open mind. Having a type, more than likely, simply means you know you like one thing, but are not open enough to move beyond that narrow set of criteria. The way one develops self-awareness is by going out into the world and having a wide variety of experiences and then learning from this broadness. There is an old sailing adage that suggests "stormy seas make able sailors." This is true of your romantic life. All those bad dates you're suffering through? Maybe it's possible to start to seeing them as steps to finding what you really want, and to getting to know yourself. And those periods of time when you cannot find a date to save your life? Well, use them to spend time exploring your life, your self, and your needs, wishes, desires, and, yes, your faults.

DO YOU LIVE TO DATE?

As a single person it's normal that dating would occupy a good deal of both your mental energy and your physical time. But many people caught on the dating treadmill spend an unhealthy amount of time involved in their dating lives. By involved I mean the time spent finding dates, the time spent actually on the date, and the mental time spent thinking about the date beforehand and obsessing over every last detail after it happens. There is no number of hours in a week that I can give you that suggests what is healthy or unhealthy. Rather, it is a matter of quality, and the effect that your dating endeavors have on the rest of your life.

Is your dating karma out of whack? Answer the following questions in your Detox Diary:

1. Have you ever cancelled plans with a friend because of a last-minute date?

2. If you find out a friend's party is unlikely to be teeming with eligible singles, does that impact your decision on whether to attend?

3. Do you find yourself skipping regular or planned activities to go on dates (such as to the gym or a social outing or an office get-together)?

4. Do your friends who are not single ever tell you that they're tired of hearing about your dating problems?

5. Are you often told you're too picky to be set up on blind dates?

6. Do you tend to get hooked on people you're not even sure you like simply because it's easier than going back "out there" and searching for someone new?

7. When you're out on a date for the first time, do you feel like you're waiting for them to "blow it" by saying something stupid? And if and when they do, are you almost relieved?

8. When someone you went on a bad date with doesn't call for a second, are you bummed out?

9. If a friend of yours tells you they met a single person who seems to have everything you're looking for, is your immediate reaction dread or despair?

10. Is your favorite part of a date when you get home to your computer to email your friends about what a joke it was?

If you answered yes to more than half of the questions above, you've got a dose of bad dating karma. Before you can go out there again, you have to make a decision that you're going to figure out what it is you truly want and whether the people you've been dating possess those key qualities. For instance, a patient of mine named Beth said she wanted someone sensitive and considerate, but would only go out with Wall Street traders who are not especially known for these softer qualities. But she liked their style and money. By limiting herself to a particular income bracket and profession, she was perpetually running on a treadmill that left her right back where she started, only more depressed and exhausted for the wear.

Take a few deep breaths and decompress.

See you tomorrow.

Day 7

As usual, begin by doing your breathing exercises, writing down all your thoughts and emotions in your Detox Diary.

Today we will be thinking about how your day-to-day activities are reflective of a healthy dating outlook. What we will be specifically examining is how much of what you do, all the time, every day, relates to your desire to meet someone or hook up, and whether it "helps" or "hurts."

Take the following example. Jen, a second-year law associate in her mid-thirties, came up with the following list for her Detox Diary:

- Drank my coffee at Starbucks instead of taking it with me (making me late for work, again) because a cute guy in a nice suit without a wedding band was sitting by the counter. (HURT)
- Didn't get a great workout at the gym during my forty-five-minute break, because I saw this good-looking guy smile at me and I was afraid if he saw me sweat he wouldn't find me attractive. (HURT)
- Didn't finish my salad at lunch because I was afraid I would get lettuce stuck between my teeth in front of the new first-year associates (hey, some of them are my age!). (HURT)
- Took a diet pill so I wouldn't wind up overeating junk food because I was so hungry from not eating lunch, but I can't afford to eat until I have a boyfriend. (HURT)
- Stayed late to finish working on a memorandum and get it off my plate rather than going out for cocktails at a bar with some friends. (HELPED)
- Cancelled dinner with two girlfriends so I could chat on an online dating service. (HURT)
- Went to sleep really late because I wound up embroiled in a chat with a guy who has absolutely none of the qualities I'm looking for in a mate. (HURT)
- Accepted a date with Mr. Never and then emailed him that on second thought I didn't want to go out with a twice-divorced car salesman whose priority was working out at the gym and going out with his buddies. (HELPED)

• Drank two glasses of wine and wrote an email to a married ex-boyfriend about how he was the best lover I ever had and to give me a call the next time he's in town on business alone. (HURT)

Now make your own list of "helpeds" and "hurts." Take a good look at your list and flesh it out. How many of the "hurts" represent recurring activities that leave you soured on dating? Do you feel like you've fallen into a regular routine that feeds off negative energy? Are you expending too much energy engaging in hurtful activities just on the outside chance of it leading to romance? If you're getting over an ex, to what extent were your hurtful activities related to that relationship? What can you do to replace hurtful activities with helpful ones? As an example, Stephanie, a graphic designer in her early thirties, did the following:

• Met a single friend for lunch and didn't once complain that "all men are cheating jackasses," even when her friend's dating woes easily warranted such a statement.
• Went to the gym at lunch and ignored the cute guy with the hot body and did a really good, sweaty workout instead.
• Cancelled attendance at a "singles party" at a downtown bar where she would have been likely to hook up with a guy at least two of her friends had already slept with.
• Made a decision to talk to her best friend about her decision to cancel their annual spring vacation together so she wouldn't miss out on a potential date with a guy she'd been seeing casually for a couple of months.
• Stopped off at a magazine shop and bought a woman's health magazine instead of a tabloid.
• Took a walk in Riverside Park by herself and sat on a bench and read without checking out the cute guys jogging by.
• Read in bed until she fell asleep at a reasonable hour.

Take a few deep breaths and decompress.
See you tomorrow.

Day 8

EXERCISE IN SELF-AWARENESS

One of the most important aspects of the Dating Detox is that it gives you a systematic template to help you focus on improving yourself. This is key because only by knowing ourselves can we know what (and who) we truly want in our lives and our beds. The goal is to make you emotionally self-sufficient and aware enough to choose your next partner for the right reasons, rather than based on insecurity and abstract ideals, and to keep you from screwing up a perfectly good relationship by subjecting your next partner to your own unresolved issues. Developing self-awareness is a lifelong pursuit. It can't be achieved in thirty days. But the tools for that kind of active exploration *can* be taught, and that is a key goal of this program.

I want you to write a totally honest dating profile of yourself, not one intended to attract others based on qualities you think are desirable, but based on who you really are and what you honestly want. For example, instead of saying you are spontaneous and primed for adventure, you might write instead that you are grumpy in the morning and need someone who will respect your space and privacy. And instead of saying you are eager to experiment in bed, you might want to say that you are not inclined to swing from chandeliers in groups of three. Write it in as much detail as possible.

Next, draft a profile of yourself from the perspective of the last person you dated with any regularity. How similar are the two profiles? Do you think you've been honest about what you want and need from a partner? To what extent are the problems you've been having related to your unwillingness to take the chance and be yourself, flaws and all? And on a more basic level, how do you think your projected self has affected your confidence and self-esteem? Do you feel as if the real you is simply too unattractive to deserve a partner? Write about your feelings in your Detox Diary. Then take a few deep breaths and decompress.

See you tomorrow.

Day 9

As always, begin with your breathing exercises.

More than likely, your dating outlook is partially the product of your childhood, adolescence, and more recent experiences, ranging from your first forays into the world of sex, dating, and romance to the last person you slept with. Since we'll be exploring your childhood in greater detail down the road, we're going to look here at how your dating history as an adult has contributed to your outlook.

Answer the following questions in your Detox Diary:

1. Racing the clock: Do you feel that you are running behind schedule compared to where you thought you'd be by this age and in comparison to your friends and peers? Where do you feel you should be in terms of mating and relating? How does this manifest itself in the ways you date and who you are willing to go out with? Do you feel like you need to make up for lost time? Are you more inclined to settle rather than wind up spending more precious time single and searching?

2. Parental/societal pressure: Does your family pressure you to settle down and get married? Do you avoid certain family functions because you are single? When you go home, do your relatives joke and nudge you about your single status? How does this make you feel?

3. Dating to get over an ex: Are you forever running on rebound? Have you experienced a heartbreak or loss that is still affecting you? Do you tend to bring this up when you're on a date? Do you compare everybody you meet to this person?

4. Just plain sick and tired of the treadmill: Are you frustrated with your current dating situation? Do all the bad dates tend to make you feel like you're somehow attracting the wrong people? When

somebody acts in an offensive manner, do you tend to internalize it as something you're bringing out in them instead of seeing it as a sign of what to avoid in the future? Do you tend to carry over feelings from bad dates into the next dates you go on?

At the end of the day, I want you to review everything you've written. Now I want you to think about your idea of the perfect date. What would the conversation be like? Where would you go? Would you know right away that this person was someone you could get serious about? Where do you think this construction of the ideal mate came from? Is it realistic? Is it based on movies and literature, a former boyfriend or girlfriend, a friend's husband or wife? Try to figure out how much of what you are looking for is based on real-life experience and how much is based on artificial constructs of the perfect mate. Take a few deep breaths and decompress.

See you tomorrow.

Day 10

Begin with your breathing exercises. Write your feelings and thoughts in your Detox Diary.

Before indulging in a little ME time, I want you to think about how you project yourself on dates, honing in on what your date may think, and what the truth of the matter actually is.

Answer the following questions from the perspective of people you've gone out with over the past several months, followed by the truth (or, at least, your view of yourself).

1. Are you easy-going or more of a type-A neurotic person?

      What your date thinks:

      The truth:

2. What are your hobbies and passions?

> What your date thinks:
>
> The truth:

3. Are you wild and spontaneous?

> What your date thinks:
>
> The truth:

4. Are you independent and self-sufficient, or are you inclined to merge your identity with a partner the moment you enter a relationship?

> What your date thinks:
>
> The truth:

5. Do you come off as needy and in a rush during the pre-dating/ first-date process?

> What your date thinks:
>
> The truth:

6. Are you willing to accept people for who they are, or do you immediately want to alter the person you're on a date with?

> What your date thinks:
>
> The truth:

7. Are you open to change and to rolling with the punches when a situation doesn't go your way?

> What your date thinks:
>
> The truth:

8. Do you make judgments based on what your date is wearing, what books they read, and/or where they went to school, or are you open to meeting (and dating) all sorts of people?

> What your date thinks:
>
> The truth:

9. Are you secure with your body and your sexuality, or do you have certain insecurities that prevent you from acting in certain ways?

What your date thinks:

The truth:

10. Are you willing to admit your faults, your foibles, and when you are wrong?

What your date thinks:

The truth:

Now it's time to go and treat yourself to some good old-fashioned ME time.

See you tomorrow.

MODULE 3: INFLUENCE AND THE INFLUENCERS
Days 11 to 15

Over the next few days we're going to look at your early life and how you were "modeled" to mate and relate. In order to create and sustain healthy relationships we need to go back to the original building blocks of your sexual and social identity. By "modeled" I mean what you learned and internalized about sex and relationships throughout your childhood and adolescence, and how those experiences formed the building blocks of a model on how to "mate and relate."

For many of us who struggle to maintain healthy intimate relationships, the seeds of our struggle can often be found in the experiences we encountered during our formative years growing up. The good news is that by exploring and understanding the experiences that form your foundation, you can constructively *remodel*. If, as you work through this module, you find that you want to delve deeper into the issues, please refer to Module 3 of the Couples' Detox on page 56, "Sexual Socialization."

Day 11

After you complete your breathing exercises, use your Detox Diary to complete the following true or false questions. Please take some time to elaborate on your answers. The purpose of this module is to explore your current capacity for intimacy by understanding your past.

1. **During my early childhood, my parents were consistently warm and affectionate toward me. True or False?**

   Please elaborate:

2. **Each parent had a different approach to intimacy. True or False?**

   Please elaborate:

3. **I have strong memories of my parents expressing affection and tenderness toward each other. True or False?**

   Please elaborate:

4. **I have positive childhood memories of my parents tucking me into bed each night. True or False?**

   Please elaborate:

5. **I have been accused by ex-partners of having certain intimacy issues. True or False?**

   Please elaborate:

6. **The following set of words best describe my approach to intimacy in serious relationships:**

   a. loving, warm, secure, tender, close, fun, trusting, comfortable, relaxing, soothing, calming, sexual, arousing, hot, tingling, playful, emotional

   b. cautious, reserved, hot and cold, up and down, somewhat anxious, guarded

   c. painful, stressful, anxious, guilty, obligatory, numb, tense, bored, tedious, annoyed

7. **When a person I am dating shares something that is truly heartfelt or secretive, I feel:**

   a. Open, warm, and interested in sharing more with them.

   b. Guarded but open-minded.

   c. Turned off and introspective.

8. I find it easy to show verbal and physical affection to friends and family, regardless of their gender or relationship to me. True or False?

Please elaborate:

9. I find it difficult to express my true feelings to people, especially those I am romantically involved with. True or False?

Please elaborate:

10. I have often looked back at relationships with a sense of regret, because I knew the person I was with wanted more from me emotionally, though I was unable to give it at the time. True or False?

Please elaborate:

In the evening, take a look through your old photo albums for snapshots from your childhood and adolescence. What do you notice about the photos? Do any of them trigger a recollection related to intimacy (or lack thereof)? In the pictures, are you and your family members physically connected or stiff and isolated? Do the photos elicit any of the thoughts and feelings you explored above? Do they trigger new associations or sensations? Do they make you wish your family had been more physically affectionate?

Select the photos that elicit the strongest reactions and place them in your memory box. Write about how they make you feel in your Detox Diary. Then take a few deep breaths and decompress.

See you tomorrow.

Day 12

We are constantly flooded with a barrage of images that tell us how to live, how to love, and whom we *should* find "attractive." Today we'll consider exactly what external forces impacted, inspired, and impeded what we find sexy and desirable. Please answer the following questions in as much detail as possible in your Detox Diary:

1. To what extent is your current dating behavior a reflection of what you learned from your parents? How much do your parents' values inform your own when it comes to your views on dating, sex, and relationships?

2. How much of what you learned about sex as a child came from what you didn't learn in school or from your parents? How much was sifted down from siblings or schoolyard gossip? To the extent you learned about sex and relationships from other kids, how much do you think those early views affect your current views? Do you still see any lingering connections to old myths? For instance, Daniel, twenty-nine, said, "When I was twelve years old, the kid who lived next door to me told me that his older brother told him that if a girl licks her lips three times in the course of conversation, she'll go to third base with you. This resulted in a number of angry responses, but its hold on my imagination persists to this day."

3. You Are What You Watch/Read: Look back at the way you answered questions about your dating fantasies in Day 4. How much of what you are looking for was formed by images from television, books, and movies? When you imagine yourself on a date, does it ever seem like a scene from a romantic comedy? A tragedy? Is there a soundtrack? When you're on a date with someone for the first time, do you find yourself evaluating him or her the way your favorite character on a sitcom would? If they use the wrong fork to eat the salad, is it a done deal? One woman I worked with, for instance, would pick her guys based on what kind of watch they wore. If it was too expensive, she figured they had serious ego issues. If it was too cheap, she thought they were probably, well, cheap. And she wasted a whole lot of time being single as a result of it. (FYI, her current partner doesn't wear a watch at all!)

At the end of the day, review everything you wrote. Now think about how all these conceptions and misconceptions have shaped your dating habits and impacted how you search for a prospective date or mate. Try to name as many people as possible that you have ruled out as a result of something you learned in childhood or picked up more recently that you know isn't true, but you can't help hearing in your head nonetheless.

Then take a few deep breaths and decompress.

See you tomorrow.

Day 13

Begin with your breathing exercises, writing down your thoughts and emotions in your Detox Diary.

Today, we are going to spend some time reflecting on how your ideas of what it means to be female and male have shaped your views.

I'd like you to begin by having you think about how your gender assumptions were modeled during your childhood.

1. Did your parents buy into gender sterotypes? Were girls and boys expected to do the same kinds of activities and chores around the house or were there exceptions based on gender?

2. Was there a double standard when it came to rules of behavior and methods of punishment and reward?

3. Looking at your parent of the same sex, to what extent do you feel you've rebelled against their gender assumptions, and to what degree have you assumed them, maybe even in spite of yourself?

4. How do gender roles affect your dating mindset? Do you feel like you have to be passive or play hard to get, or conversely, do you feel some pressure to take the lead?

If these issues are too abstract to fathom, consider the following statements, each of which bristles with a thorny stereotype or three. Without censoring yourself for political correctness, on a gut level, do

you agree or disagree? Go through the statements quickly. In your Detox Diary, write down an "A" (for agree) or "D" (for disagree) for each
statement.

1. If you are single and dating it's okay to split the check.

2. Men should always pay on a date.

3. Men typically have more sexual experience than women.

4. Men should take the lead sexually.

5. On a date, a guy should make the first move.

6. A woman should play hard to get.

7. Women play games and lead men on.

8. Women use sex to manipulate men.

9. Men are logical; women are emotional.

10. Women cry to manipulate men.

11. It's okay for men to stare at women or make comments.

12. Women should take male attention as a form of flattery.

13. During sex, men get overwhelmed with passion and might get
rough.

14. Men are better at sports.

15. Men don't cry. Men don't feel.

16. Men have more notches in their belt.

17. A woman should be careful about revealing her "number" (of past sexual partners) to a man.

18. Sexual prowess is a sign of masculinity.

19. In every man there's a little boy.

20. A woman needs a man to be happy.

21. A man needs a woman to take care of him.

22. When a guy gets sexually excited, he can't be put off.

23. If a woman sexually excites a man and doesn't deliver, she's a tease.

24. Men are more violent and easier to excite than women.

25. Men use sex as a bargaining tool.

26. Women should dress provocatively to excite a man.

27. When single and dating, a woman should cancel plans with female friends for the opportunity to be with a man.

28. A gay person can change his sexual orientation if he or she really wants to.

29. A man's "number" should never be less than a woman's.

30. If a guy pays for a date, he deserves or expects some sexual attention in return.

31. If a woman doesn't go to bed with a guy after a couple of dates, she's probably a prude.

32. If a woman goes to bed with a guy on the first date, she's easy.

33. If a woman is hanging out at a bar, either with friends or alone, she's looking to have a good time and should expect male attention.

34. A gay man is not a real man.

35. A gay woman is not a real woman.

36. Men take risks; women play it safe.

37. Men are thrill-seekers; women are creatures of comfort.

38. If a man is insulted, he needs to stand up for himself.

39. If a man's girlfriend is insulted, he needs to stand up for her.

40. A woman who's a lesbian just hasn't had a real man to set her straight.

Of the forty statements, how many did you find yourself agreeing with? One or two, a bunch, more than half? For all the statements you found yourself agreeing with, where do you think these gender assumptions come from? Your parents? Your friends? The media?

How have gender assumptions shown themselves in your dating and relationship history? Look at your last serious relationship as a starting point for thinking about how gender assumptions shaped the way you engaged with each other both in and out of bed. At times, did you find yourself feeling like you had to conform to ideas of what was manly or womanly? Write it all down in your Detox Diary.

Then take a few deep breaths and decompress.

See you tomorrow.

Day 14

Begin with your breathing exercises, trying to relax and focus. Write down your emotions and thoughts in your Detox Diary.

In Part I, Chapter 4 (see page 22), we discussed how to replace negative habits and thoughts with positive ones by leveraging your brain's natural propensity to rewire itself through a process known as neuroplasticity. In order to access your brain's potential to do this, you're going to use a system I've dubbed reORDERing in which you **O**bserve how outside influences have shaped your behaviors, **R**ecognize recurring patterns and what triggers them, **De**-couple your responses from those triggers, **E**ngage in healthier behaviors, and **R**egulate yourself as you move forward with a new sense of awareness.

To reORDER successfully you need to be able to reflect upon all of the external factors that shaped and influenced your dating outlook, and to connect your current behaviors to these earlier experiences. To begin, I am going to ask you to imagine the following hypothetical situation:

You are at a party when an attractive person comes up to you and starts a conversation. It seems you have a fair amount in common. You walk out of the party together. What are the thoughts that immediately run through your head? Check all that apply.

- Should I sleep with him or her?

- How much money does he or she make?

- If he or she's so great, why isn't he or she already taken?

- Is he or she just interested in sex?

- Maybe this is "the one."

- This will be a great story to tell our kids one day.

- What's wrong with him or her?

- Can I go in late to work tomorrow?

- Oh no, what if he or she's a smoker/Scientologist/unemployed bum/Republican/Democrat/vegetarian/fill in the blank?

How did you respond? What are the expectations and pressures you place early on in a potential romantic situation, and where do they come from? How are they affecting your ability to connect in a positive way?

Laura, a thirty-two-year-old retail buyer who had come to see me after one too many hook-ups and heartbreaks, described a recent encounter with a guy:

"I met him at a party, and he asked if he could walk me home. Of course, I said yes. Then he kissed me. So I asked him if he wanted to come upstairs. One thing led to another, and we made our way to the couch. This led to the bedroom. We had sex. It was amazing. Or at least he thought it was amazing, because I faked it to make him feel really good about himself. He spent the night and I made him breakfast the next morning. He didn't ask for my number, so I just gave him my business card and told him to call me. He didn't. I asked my friend from the party for his contact information and I called him. But he never responded. I guess I made it too easy for him, or maybe he thought I was a slut. Plus my friend said he was an advertising executive, so I'm sure he can have any woman he wants, so why would he bother with me? If I hadn't slept with him, he would have lost interest anyway. The whole thing is obviously hopeless. I don't know how anyone ever winds up in a relationship."

Okay, let's apply the process of reORDERing to Laura's situation to see what influenced her decisions and what she could have done differently:

OBSERVE: Says Laura: "I grew up thinking that men only want one thing and in order to keep them around, you'd better give it to them or somebody else will. This is what my mom did (she's still single and dating) and what all my close friends have been doing since high school."

RECOGNIZE: Says Laura: "I always wind up sleeping with men too quickly, because I get scared that they won't be interested in seeing me again otherwise. I feel as if what I've got going for me is that I've got a good body and I'm pretty hot in bed, or at least I always put on a good show. So I figure I should play to my strengths. But when I stop to think about it on a deeper level, I recognize that this stems from insecurity, and my belief that my best qualities as a potential mate have to do with externals. I have lots of great female friends who say I'm really kind and nurturing, and I'm spontaneous and fun to be around. So I should learn to trust that there are at least some men who would value these qualities too. I guess it comes down to a lot of what I learned about sex from watching my mother. She was always dating different guys and always bringing them home and always focused on trying to look like a teenager herself."

DE-COUPLE: "Next time I'm walking home with a guy and I start worrying that I'll never see them again if I don't put out, I'm going to recognize that it's my fear and insecurity speaking, and not necessarily the situation at hand. . . . I don't have to act like my mother, or worry that I'm going to end up like her. I'm my own person, so I need to have the confidence to make my own decisions and do what's right for me. . . . Worst case scenario is I don't have to wash my sheets the next day."

ENGAGE: "Next time I go out on a date, if I like the guy I'll kiss him goodnight, and leave him wanting more, and have confidence that he will want to see me again. This will let him know that I have more to offer than a night of sex, and I'm actually interested in getting to know someone and have a meaningful relationship."

REGULATE: "This is going to be the tough part: to stick with this attitude. What if he doesn't call me, or I call him and he doesn't call me back? It may feel like I made a mistake, and I'll be tempted to go back to my old ways. But I just have to be willing to know what I want and to hold out for my bigger goals, or it may never happen. The hardest part is being alone. I always use sex as a way of avoiding being alone in bed. But now that I have a better understanding of where my insecurity and low self-esteem come from, I don't think I'll be as afraid of being alone."

Now it's your turn. Write down a typical dating scenario, whether it's one like Laura's that always ends in hooking up, or otherwise: Maybe you're commitment-phobic and avoid dating anyone you might really like, or maybe you only date one "type" of person, or maybe you don't date at all, or are afraid of trying new things to meet someone. Write down the scenario, and then take the time to ruminate and fill in a re-ORDERing chart as it applies to the scenario. What can you observe? What patterns do you recognize? Where do you think they come from, and how can you de-couple those present-day behaviors from any underlying fears, anxieties, and issues that are based in the past. Once you have this knowledge, how will it change the ways you engage when you're out on a date, and what core values and affirmative beliefs will you need to hold onto in order to regulate and maintain a path toward positive growth?

Take a few deep breaths and decompress.

See you tomorrow.

Day 15

At this point you are halfway through the Detox. Take a moment to congratulate yourself.

Without reviewing your diary or even thinking too much about this, name three things you will do differently when either choosing a mate or going out on your next date.

Write out a list of dating goals or commandments for the next twelve months. Keep in mind that "fall in love and get married" is a lovely aspiration, but it's not a goal. What I'm talking about is more along the lines of:

- I will not judge the merits or faults of a date within the first three minutes.

- I will not have sex with someone solely to sustain their interest.

- I will not pretend I am easy-going when I am totally type-A, since it makes me act phony and keeps me from connecting.

- I will not pretend I read Russian literature when I prefer to watch reality television, since I wouldn't even date myself based on the pretentious way I portray myself.

Now get out there and enjoy some ME time.
See you tomorrow.

MODULE 4: HOW YOU DATE
Days 16 to 20

In this, the fourth module, we are going to explore how you date. We are going to look at and challenge the ways you search for prospective partners, how you go about selecting and arranging dates, and how you act during and after the actual dates themselves. Basically, we are going to strip down your tired old dating habits and rebuild them to be more consistent with your long-term romantic goals.

Day 16

Begin with your breathing exercises. Write down your thoughts and feelings in your Detox Diary.

Today, we will begin at the beginning of the dating process. In order to see yourself as you really are, you need to create an accurate snapshot of how you handle yourself throughout the process. To do this, we will re-create various scenarios that end with you on a date. As a first step, think back to the last five dates you have had (either with one person, or five separate dates if the former doesn't apply).

1. How did these dates come about? How did you meet this person(s)?

2. What was the form of initial contact? And how long did it take between the initial contact and the date?

3. Where did you go and what did you do? Did you come up with a planned activity? Was it what you would have ideally wanted to do? Was it dinner and a movie when you would have preferred a picnic and a hike?

4. Did you meet during the day or the night?

5. If you felt some chemistry, what was it that you liked about the person? Was this reciprocated? How was this shown?

6. If you didn't click with the person, what about them left you cold? Did you go through with the entire date? Would you go out with them again nonetheless?

7. Was there any follow-up? What was it like?

ENGAGEMENT EXERCISE

Look back at your date book or calendar and see how many dates you've been on in the past six months. Then look back at the email communications that preceded and followed your dates (and try to think about the verbal communications that went along with them). Do you see any distinct patterns? When you reread your own words or remember how much effort went into them, does it seem silly and pointless? A waste of energy? Was it emotional overkill? In retrospect, try to write down how you felt at the time. Even if you weren't crazy about the person, how much energy did you invest in the dating process anyway? And if there was a connection, what happened?

Now go back and think about what you could have done differently. Did you inject too much pressure and negativity into the interaction? Did you sell yourself short by trying too hard or not being yourself? Did you try too hard even though you really weren't interested? How did it turn out? Did you wind up losing the upper hand in a situation you weren't all that excited about to begin with?

At the end of the day, I want you to reread your answers above, and then I want you to rewrite history. Think back on those date(s) and write about what you wish had happened. Maybe you walked out on them during the entrée when they leered at someone at the next table or checked their BlackBerry for the zillionth time. Or maybe you kissed them at the table, even though it isn't something you typically do in public, let alone on a first date. Let your imagination literally get the best of you.

Then spend a little time thinking about "what you did" versus "what you wish you had done" and write down the reasons that stopped you from taking action. For example: Brian, thirty-two, went on a couple of dates with a woman, Kristy, who he was really attracted to and would have liked to have continued dating, but she wasn't of the same religion. Brian considered himself a nonconformist who didn't believe in organized religion, but nonetheless felt that he should only seriously date women of the same religion as himself. He ended up blowing Kristy off without any explanation, and later regretted the decision quite a bit. In doing this exercise, he realized that what prevented him from taking action in the way he would have liked was a serious fear of disappointing his parents, to the point where he often dated women that his parents liked more than he did.

Take a few deep breaths and decompress.

See you tomorrow.

Day 17

After you finish your breathing exercises, we are going to look at how you meet people and the behaviors you exhibit before the date even begins. In many ways, the actions and emotions that guide this aspect of your dating life are a good indication of your level of "dating health." If you find yourself anxious when you don't have dates, or if you spend more time fretting about what could go wrong on an upcoming date than happily anticipating a pleasant evening, that's an indication that things could be healthier. Moreover, if you spend more waking hours looking for dates than doing everything else put together (including hanging out with friends and family and engaging in hobbies), then the long and short of it is this: Just like the Run-D.M.C. song, "You Be Illin'."

IS DATING YOUR JOB?

Look back at how you spent the last few weeks of your dating life before you undertook this program. How much of your dating life was spent on what I would call "dating logistics"? By this I mean, how much time did you spend surfing online dating sites, going to parties and bars on the off-chance of meeting someone, hanging out in the hardware store, or sitting at the bookstore cafe pretending to read, all in the hopes of meeting someone? In short, how much mental energy did you put into your love life?

ARE YOUR NUMBERS UP?

Look back on the number of dates you went on over the past six months (if you can't recall, this alone may be an indication of "overdating"). As you assess these dates, how many of these were first dates that didn't go anywhere? Do you feel as if they're all blurring together? Can you remember the first and last names of all the people you went out with over the last six months? How many of the "no ways" did you fool around with or sleep with and then fret about afterward even though you knew you really weren't interested? Do you approach dating and mating the way you did getting into college? Are there back ups and safeties, long shots and early decisions? How much of what you do before and after a specific date has to do with how you actually feel about the person and their potential as either a long-term prospective partner or even a casual fling? Do you feel like you're so lost in a game of statistical probability that you no longer know what or who you want?

DIGITAL DEXTERITY

Do you meet most of the people you date in the real world or online? If online, how often do you check your date-mail during the workday? When you get a note saying new folks have registered who match your general criteria, does your heart skip a click? Do you find yourself quickly jotting a note to them without even reading through their profile thoroughly just to get a jump on the competition? How often do you contact (or return notes from) people who don't have any photos on their profile? When you think about all the mail sitting in your box unopened from new prospective dates, does it make you giddy? What do you think you are missing by not being online? On the whole, are your current behaviors bringing you closer to finding a suitable partner? Can you come up with a more constructive list of ways to meet new people outside of ordinary channels like online dating, work, bars, or parties where the same group of people is likely to attend? For instance, joining a book club, starting a film club by posting an ad on Craigslist, getting involved with a local charity, going on ski weekends or camping trips with an environmental tour group, or perhaps joining the local chapter of your alumni association or getting involved with fundraising for an art gallery or museum . . . even joining a new gym in a different neighborhood?

Make a list of ten ways you can expand your existing social circle. Remember that even if you believe that "most of the good ones are already married or taken," meeting new people gets you in touch with a whole new network of their friends, some of whom are bound to be single. So don't be so quick to judge or rule out new avenues for extending your existing social boundaries.

Take a few deep breaths and decompress.

See you tomorrow.

Day 18

After you finish your breathing exercises, we are going to spend some time looking at your behavior while you are out on dates.

For many of us, dating has become a task, like grocery shopping. For others, it's a game, where the object is to win the interest of the other person, even if we don't much like them. And there we sit with our lists and score sheets, checking off traits and doing a quick tally in our heads.

Write down your answers to the following questions in your Detox Diary:

1. Do you feel as if you are "good" at dating? Has it become a competitive sport in which you've trained yourself how to avoid the pitfalls like a seasoned Olympian? How does this interfere with your ability to experience the date while it is happening? Are you more interested in the sport than the person you are sitting across from?

2. Do you typically try to "get through" the date and then decide whether you actually liked the person after? Is this a fact-gathering mission or an act of social interaction?

3. How do you decide whether or not you like the person? Is it based on actual chemistry or how well they measured up to your running checklist? Do you find you are often doing an exit interview by the time you get to dessert?

4. By the time you are an hour into the date, have you already decided whether you would sleep with this person and/or have his/her babies? Once you reach a tentative decision, how much does it influence your ability to see past your first impressions?

5. How often do you engage in sexual activity just out of obligation? How often is it to hold the person's interest, to be competitive within this "do-me" dating market? How much does that affect your ability to remember whether or not you actually liked the person? Do you find yourself getting attached after the fact based on engaging in sexual activity you weren't all that sure you wanted in the first place?

Just as Supreme Court Justice Stewart opined in defining obscenity, most people claim they know the difference between lust and love at first sight, saying things like "I know it when I see it." These sorts of snap decisions, in turn, drive dating behavior to unforeseen destinations. If they don't immediately "feel it" for the person, in their heads they write them off. If they do see something based on some odd combination of checked-off items on their laundry list of love must-haves, they will throw good energy after bad in trying to make it work.

Try to recall two instances where mistaken first impressions (you know, the sort you project) led you to pursue a person who really wasn't all that great and made you rule out a person for reasons just as premature or spurious. Think about what exactly led you to make such a ruling. Then think about how you wish both of those situations would have gone instead.

Write a few key phrases regarding how and why you formed those snap judgments. Then take a few deep breaths and decompress.

See you tomorrow.

Day 19

After you do your deep breathing exercises, we will be devoting some time today to how we react after the date is over. How do we debrief ourselves from the onslaught of hormones, pheromones, excitement, and disappointment that defined the date and then decide what it is we want? A lot of the single people I work with often say that a first date is more like a car crash than a social outing. Before they know it, it's over and they're left feeling numbed and bruised and unsure who is liable for the damages. Are you so numb from dating that you can't even tell the good dates from the bad?

Ask yourself some of the following questions:

1. How strongly are you tied to rigid gender assumptions that leave you waiting for the other person to make the first/next move?

2. Do you tend to get caught up in a spiral of insecurity and mixed emotions that leads you to forget that you really didn't like the person to begin with?

3. Do you generally spend so much time reviewing what went right or wrong on a date such that you neglect to spend enough time considering whether you actually clicked with the person? How

much of your reaction to a date will depend on what your friends think when you go over how the person measured up to your checklist? Do you find that discussing a date too soon after with your friends kills your sense of romance and passion? Are some friends more negative, pessimistic, cynical, and ultimately toxic than others? Going forward, are there some friends that should be removed from your dating-analysis circle?

Write down at least two things you did or didn't do after each of your last five dates and what you could have done instead. For instance, let's say there was someone who you really liked who didn't write or call you right away, and then by the time they did, you had worked yourself into such an emotional frenzy that it killed all good feelings toward the possibility of a relationship. Write about what you wish you would have done differently.

Or, on the other hand, if someone you liked never did get in touch with you and you didn't have the guts to get in touch with them and it left you wondering how on earth you could have had such a different reaction, write about that. Why didn't you contact them? What would you have said?

At the end of the day, reread what you've written and come up with a few new ground rules. For instance, "if I like someone, I will call them." Or, "if I don't like someone, I will not go out with them again." Then take a few deep breaths and decompress.

See you tomorrow.

Day 20

It's the end of another module, which means you're going to get a little ME time.

For today's activity, go somewhere where you're likely to find a lot of singles. If you live in a small community and you want to avoid running into people you know, hey, I get it. But go somewhere else. I don't care if it's a gym or a park or a bar or anywhere else where singles are likely to gather. And I want you to not dress up. When you go home, write about how it makes you feel. Did you feel insecure and unattractive? Did you feel anxious that other single folks were getting more positive attention? Think about it and write about it in detail. How much energy and ego are you investing in getting small insignificant tokens of attention from potential mates? How much does this feed your ego and deplete your energy? How much is your own sense of self-worth dependent on the proverbial kindness of others?

Congratulations. You have finished another key module.

See you tomorrow.

MODULE 5: WHAT DO YOU WANT IN A PARTNER?

Days 21 to 25

Earlier in the Detox we looked at the qualities people consider when assessing and evaluating a mate. These factors typically include **physical attractiveness, intelligence, social standing,** and **personality.** The combination of these dimensions generally forms your impression of someone's overall appeal. While we may weigh certain attributes above others, most people look at these four basic elements. The problem some people develop after a long period of dating is that they get too closely focused on various aspects of this checklist and don't allow for sufficient compromise. I'm not suggesting that you should settle regarding something that's genuinely important to you, but the point of this program is to help you learn the difference between settling and being open-minded, as well as learn to tear down the barriers that prevent you from seeing all the options.

As we learned in analyzing the early influences that shaped our models of romantic attachment, we often base what we think we want on values we've never truly taken the time to question. And when it comes right down to it, we frequently repeat the patterns we learned from our parents and formative experiences regardless of whether they fulfill our sexual and emotional needs. By utilizing the method of retracing and rewiring, it is my hope that when you come out of the detox program and begin to date again, you will explore what and who you want with a fresh set of eyes and develop healthier patterns of behavior consistent with your long-term relationship goals.

Day 21

After you complete your breathing exercises, we will begin this, our penultimate module, by examining those characteristics we *believe* we want and need in a mate.

In your Detox Diary, write down the list of characteristics that you consider the most important in selecting a prospective mate, using the four broad dimensions listed above—physical attractiveness, intelligence, social standing, and personality—as your guides. Go ahead and be as specific as your tastes warrant. If you feel blue eyes and olive skin are essential, say so. If an upbeat, outgoing personality is key, describe what you mean. If religious background is important, indicate it. If a particular profession is either an automatic yes or no, jot that down as well.

After you have listed as many traits as possible, think about which of these qualities are most important to you. For some it is a particular emotional sensibility, while for others intellect is the priority. Have you ever met the person you described? How much of this list plays through your head when you're out on a first date or you meet someone at a party? Are there some qualities you try to be flexible about that are simply deal-breakers? Are there others you may think are crucial that, when it comes down to it, are less often factors into who you find attractive? How many of these qualities can you determine on the first date? Do you tend to form snap decisions about someone's desirability without knowing the full facts? How much of your list is based on interior aspects of attraction and compatibility, and how much extends from environmental cues, such as what you think your peers would think of a particular person?

As an example, I worked with a woman named Marsha, a thirty-two-year-old real estate lawyer who had no trouble meeting men. She was a successful associate in a medium-sized firm and had a very active social life. Her work brought her in contact with a large number of eligible men, who often asked her out. She also made a point of socializing in lots of different circles, some affiliated with her college, some her law school, some having to do with long-distance biking, which was her passion, and others ranging from wine-tasting to charitable activities. Marsha was somewhat reluctant to give up her carefree single life, but felt that given her desire to have children, the time had come to get serious. And being a focused object-oriented professional, once she made that decision, she came to me seeking a clear-cut plan in order to realize her relationship goals. When I asked Marsha to outline the qualities she was looking for in a mate, her initial list looked as follows:

Physical Attractiveness

- thick brown hair, some gray is okay, but absolutely no baldies, hair-plugs, or receding hairlines!
- blue, hazel, or green eyes
- at least 5'9" tall
- athletic, lean build
- not overly muscled or buff
- deep speaking voice, no outer-borough accents or snorting laughter
- nice clothes, but not foppish or flashy
- olive complexion, no freckles
- no facial hair
- nice smile

Intelligence

- a master's degree or better, preferably from an Ivy League school
- must be able to engage in witty banter at lightning speed
- well-read and articulate
- ability to speak another language a strong plus
- prefer an IQ above 162

Social Standing

- Ivy-educated
- extremely successful professionally
- should be involved with at least one charity

Personality

- passionate
- open-minded and tolerant
- generous
- outgoing
- confident and spontaneous
- witty, especially in social settings
- responsible
- driven and goal-oriented
- progressive politically
- never sexist or racist or otherwise embarrassing
- impeccable table manners

EXPANDING YOUR HORIZONS

Now write out a list of the qualities you find important in a friend. What are the major differences in your two "ideal personas"? What are the similarities? Does your friend list contain less specificity? Do your closest friends meet most of the criteria you laid out?

Marsha's list looked like this:

Physical Attractiveness

- couldn't care less: I don't judge my friends by how they look. But I tend to choose friends who are interested in being the best they can be, which means healthy and fit. And I don't like slackers!

Intelligence

- extremely insightful, analytical, and intellectual
- funny and witty
- well-educated, though not necessarily in a traditional way
- original thinker
- stimulating conversationalist

Social Standing

• either holds down a professional job or did before having kids
• must have achieved some level of success and/or still aspire to

Personality

• smart and cerebral
• funny, scathing sense of humor
• loyal
• honest
• reliable
• open-minded and nonjudgmental
• warm, but not overly emotional
• optimistic and goal-oriented
• good values

As Marsha compared her lists, she realized that the key areas that mattered to her were the ones that appeared on both her lists. She learned that as much as she thought she cared about appearance and professional status, what mattered most to her was intelligence, a sense of humor, open-mindedness, a sense of optimism, a strong work ethic, and a drive toward general self-betterment. In other words, "no slackers or idiots. I want someone who is stimulating intellectual company and will challenge my views and opinions about myself and the world, someone who is internally driven to do whatever he does with passion and determination."

Upon reaching this conclusion, Marsha realized that how tall a man was or whether he had a graduate degree from Harvard or an undergrad degree from a state college didn't matter to her nearly as much as how passionate and driven he was. This allowed her to understand why so many of her dates had left her bored to pieces even though they possessed many of the qualities she was looking for. By learning to look for "internal passion" as opposed to "external success," Marsha was ultimately able to widen her dating scope and start meeting men she really clicked with on a deeper level.

Now analyze your own lists. How often have you been bored or left cold by people that match what you think are your key criteria? Think about why.

Write down the qualities you realize are not that important to you. Then take a few deep breaths and decompress.

See you tomorrow.

Day 22

Continuing where we left off yesterday, we're going to focus on that little thing we can't do without no matter how much we dig witty conversation and a positive outlook on life. Yup, physical attraction. Sure, it's all well and good to leave ourselves open to change and possibility. But c'mon. You can't manufacture being hot for someone. And believe me, I'm the last person in the world to make you try. So today we're going to think beyond all those other dimensions we talked about yesterday, such as fertile minds, charitable giving, and Ivy League educations. Today we're going to think about what it is about someone that turns us on, at a gut level.

Let's assume, for argument's purpose, that you have moved beyond your preconceived notions and your parents' values and your formative forays and figured out those qualities you really must have in a prospective mate. Now, what transforms that person from a good friend into someone you could fall in love with?

Write down the names of three people on whom you have had wicked crushes at some point in your life. These need not necessarily be people you got involved with, though that might have happened. Using those same four dimensions we discussed yesterday, think about how you'd describe your three biggest crushes.

For instance, Marsha came up with the following list:

1. Todd (junior year of high school): skinny, pale, dark sense of humor, weird, offbeat, liked Black Sabbath.

2. Jeff (sophomore year of college): chubby, tan, math major, played Dungeons and Dragons, dark sense of humor, eccentric hobbies like archery, liked The Smiths.
3. Peter (two years ago): average height/build, designed video games, scathing sense of humor, dark streak, played hockey, liked Zeppelin.

So what do all these guys from Marsha's past have in common? It wasn't the olive complexion she ostensibly preferred or the master's degree or professional success she'd ticked off on her checklist. Nope, it was a scathing sense of humor. And once Marsha thought about it, she realized that while several of her other long-term partners had possessed most of the qualities she'd ostensibly desired, they hadn't had that dark scathing wit that truly made her melt.

Now it's your turn. Thinking back on those three biggest crushes, what are the first qualities that come to mind when you think about them? Try not to consider your usual laundry list. Instead, see if you can remember their most prominent traits or characteristics, the ones that made them so totally unique and that first pop into your mind upon the very mention of the their names.

After you're done, circle the traits they have in common and/or the ones that seem related or similar and see what you come up with.

Now take a few deep breaths and decompress.

See you tomorrow.

Day 23

After you've completed your breathing exercises and written down your thoughts and emotions, we will begin tackling that murky thing called relationship history. Most of us would rather eat leftovers three days in a row than tread this mucky swamp, but it's important to divorce yourself of those romanticized memories of "the one that got away" and remember, "Hey, wait a minute, wasn't that the jackass who did my best friend while I was in Kansas City for an executive management conference on networking synergy?" So put on your wetsuit, because we're going to wade through the swamp for a bit.

ARE YOU HAUNTED BY GHOSTS OF RELATIONSHIPS PAST?

Many single people find that they get caught up in a relationship from their past, usually a difficult break up or a situation where something ended badly. Often, these relationships become romanticized, expanding to dangerously idealistic proportions. Such baggage can make it difficult for a person to move ahead, because no real person can compete with the perfect ghost. These ghosts become a defensive means to avoid getting attached and putting ourselves at risk again. Even if we think we've gotten over someone and put up the obligatory smoke screen of bawdy expletives about what a "two-timing [fill in the blank] he or she was," they may be hanging in our mental closets, dampening our excitement about whatever or whomever else we try on for size.

Today, I want you to list the names of your absolute worst breakups, the ones who still linger in your mind, the ones who you still Google for current information, the ones who piss you off and depress you as the biggest wastes of your precious dating time. Think about the qualities that drew you to them. Also, if they were the ones who soured on the relationship or, worse, if they left you for someone else, think about the qualities they were searching for that you did not ostensibly possess.

For instance, Mark, a thirty-four-year-old investment banker, came to me after two years of pining over an ex, saying he couldn't meet anyone else who came close. His ex, Bridget, had left him, claiming she needed to "do her own thing," but when he looked her up online a few months later, he learned she was already engaged to another guy, who was nothing like him. As it turned out, his list of what initially attracted him to Bridget was not as important as her description of the man she left him for, for those qualities had become hardened into his psyche as not only qualities he pretended to possess, but also qualities he specifically avoided in seeking out a potential mate, simply because the thought of giving them that sort of power over him again made him too angry.

Let me be specific. According to Mark, the guy Bridget ultimately married was unlike him in that he was "extremely physically fit, tawny, outdoorsy, spontaneous, non-materialistic, mellow, free-spirited and flaky/sensitive." Upon making this list, Mark realized that he'd subsequently gone out of his way to pretend to be some of these things. He found that he'd even avoided going out with anyone who possessed any of these traits, although a few of them were a key part of his "must-haves": free-spirited, spontaneous, and non-materialistic were terms that all came up in his "three wicked crushes" list.

By going back and de-coupling these qualities from the negative context, Mark was able to reclaim them as traits he did not, in fact, possess, but which, in some part, represented things he was looking for in an ideal mate.

Now it's your turn. When you're done writing about what you liked and hated about your ex or exes and what you think they were looking for, can you see any similarities with your own lists of wants and dislikes, of absolute no-nos?

At the end of the day, review what you've written and jot down those traits you truly crave in a mate. It's time to bury those skeletons in your closet once and for all and re-experience the bliss of warm flesh. Chances are when you get down to it, that ex of yours did not have all the qualities you truly wanted, but had the qualities you thought you wanted. And when you get back out there the next time, you'll seek out a person who's just right for you. So it's time to let go of the phantoms and return to the world of the living. Now take a few deep breaths and decompress.

See you tomorrow.

Day 24

Today, after we complete our breathing exercises, we're going to do an exercise in letting go. Part of the process of becoming a successful, toxin-free dater is learning to let go. As with so many aspects of life, you cannot control how someone else is going to react to you, and you cannot control their feelings or actions. In many ways, the goal of the Detox is to teach you to be mindful and present but to let go of those things you cannot control.

That is to say, you need to put your best foot forward with every date you go on, and you need to have the confidence to know that if it doesn't work out, it's okay. Dwelling, hoping, pining, and doing all of those other anxiety-ridden post-date behaviors will only make you less happy. So, for this exercise, we are going to work on our "letting go" skills.

Start by writing down five or ten things that bother you about your dating life. I'm talking about specific instances where you feel your heart was broken, or your feelings were hurt, or where you felt something for someone and it was not reciprocated. List these events and briefly describe how they made you feel.

Now write down what you think "caused" this to happen. How many times did you list yourself as a cause?

Now try to recall what you can of that person, their values and their character. Write down any flaws you noticed, or anything they did that you feel was "wrong."

Going over this list, does it seem possible that whatever happened had nothing to do with you? Moreover, you are still here, alive and well! Whatever these things were, doesn't it seem like you blew them out of proportion at the time? Can you see how letting them go right then and there might have saved you needless heartache and despair?

See you tomorrow.

Day 25

As we approach the end of another module, it's time to engage in a little ME time. Today, I'd like you to go somewhere you wouldn't ordinarily go to meet someone based on the new criteria you elaborated for a desired mate. In other words, if you usually go to a particular neighborhood teeming with the kinds of people you are unlikely to click with, then go somewhere new instead. If you usually go to a tragically hip downtown bar where you've misconnected with the majority of your recent dates, today why not try an uptown park or museum? If time permits, how about a whole new scene altogether, maybe a cafe or live music venue in a nearby town or city?

Expanding your dating horizons is often as simple as hopping on the subway or driving an extra twenty minutes. You are not going to try to pick someone up, of course. But I want you to look around and get a sense of all the people you haven't been meeting simply by traveling in the same narrow circles over and over again.

Maybe you're a little sad and frustrated at just how much time you feel like you've wasted in going out with the same old wrong people over and over again. But hopefully you are also charged with eager excitement, ready to get back out there with renewed vision and a grander purview of your ideal mate.

Congratulations, you are one final step short from achieving a less toxic, healthier and happier way of dating and relating!

See you tomorrow.

MODULE 6: READY, STEADY, GO!
Days 26 to 30

The final module for your Dating Detox is designed to get you ready to date again. This time, I hope, you'll get out there with a different outlook, a new set of eyes, and a much improved mindset. If the Detox has been successful, you will have changed the way you search, what you're looking for and how you react when a date doesn't work out. You may go through additional periods of not dating, and you may find yourself wanting and needing self-imposed breaks. But all of this will be done with the knowledge that you have something unique to offer, and that a whole bevy of potential mates are out there just waiting to meet someone exactly like you.

What all these things add up to is your readiness. When I talk about readiness, I don't necessarily mean readiness to date, though that is certainly a part of the equation. Rather, readiness means the ability and maturity to be in a long-term relationship. It takes the right sort of dating mindset to get to such a place, so, for this reason, readiness covers both dating and the ensuing relationship. In other words, if you are just dating to find new sexual partners or because you enjoy meeting new people, but have no deeper desire to commit, you are likely not "ready." This is not to say that having casual flings is bad. It can be precisely what you want or need at the moment. But what we have been working toward is how to identify (and, of course, find and keep) a prospective long-term mate.

Day 26

After you complete your breathing exercises, I'm going to give you a "readiness quiz." As with the quiz you took on Day 1 of the Detox, this is less about attaining a "good score" and more about getting you to think about what you truly want and where you are in terms of those things you desire. Write down answers to the following questions in your Detox Diary. These are not true/false or multiple choice questions. Rather, I want you to answer yes or no to each of the following statements and elaborate on what it means to you.

1. I am open to the possibility of changing my expectations in order to embrace a serious relationship.

2. I am willing to take stock of my previous patterns and approach dating in a new and healthier way.

3. I am aware that some of the things I've been looking for have been influenced by baggage from my childhood and previous relationships.

4. I believe there is more than one "ideal mate" per person, and a good partner is not defined by a list of achievements and traits, but by being willing and able to commit to making the relationship work.

5. I will not project who I am and what I want in ways that are at odds with my true desires based on fulfilling some mainstream ideal of what the "perfect lover" is supposed to be like.

6. I will not be unduly influenced by the opinions of friends and family when it comes to knowing who and what I want in a potential mate.

7. I will not regard myself as incomplete when I'm not in a relationship.

8. I will not settle for someone who does not make me happy out of fear of being alone/single.

9. I will make an ongoing effort to consider whether a person might be right before disqualifying them based on initial decisions or snap judgements.

10. I will explore new avenues and expand my social horizons to meet new people.

If you were able to answer yes to all of the above "ten dating commandments," then you are already on the cusp of embarking on a healthier path.

If you found yourself answering no to any of the questions, take the time to explore those answers more deeply in your Detox Diary.

At the end of the day, please review your answers to the questions above, especially those that gave you pause. Perhaps you still feel that modifying your existing list of dating criteria would be "compromising" or "settling," due to how you think your friends or family might react to potential mates. If so, spend some time thinking about what it is (and who it is) that is holding you back from finding people who possess the qualities you truly want. Are you worried that your unhappily married best friend who is on the verge of divorcing a name partner in a law firm would disapprove if you dated a high school English teacher? Do your best to question yourself, even if what you discover doesn't sit well with your own conceptions about yourself. Write down whatever key issues come to mind that positively or negatively affect your ability to commit to finding a compatible mate. Then take a few deep breaths and decompress.

See you tomorrow.

Day 27

After you finish your morning breathing exercises, we're going to take a look at how history has repeated itself with regard to your ability to make a relationship work and the difficulties that you have faced during your relationships. Consider these five pivotal milestones in dating someone new:

1. The first date
2. Anticipation of the second and third dates when you think there might be something there
3. Sex with a prospective partner for the first time
4. Your new partner meeting your friends and family
5. Your first big fight

In assessing each of these milestones in a new relationship, think about each one through the following lenses and how they might have negatively impacted the milestone. Pick the lenses/areas that most apply based on the work we've been doing throughout the Detox:

A. Family values
B. Early socialization: insecurity/fear of rejection
C. Formative firsts: pressure to put out/perform
D. Previous relationships
E. Current dating patterns

As an example, Olivia, a divorced thirty-seven-year-old behavioral psychologist, completed her first entry as follows:

1. THE FIRST DATE

A. FAMILY VALUES: I'm a failure! I should be married with kids by now; I may wind up an old maid; if the guy seems as if he would be a good provider and is ready to be in a relationship, I have to try to make it work by all means possible (even if that means misrepresenting myself on various levels)!

B. EARLY SOCIALIZATION: INSECURITY/FEAR OF REJECTION: If I were really good looking and desirable, I wouldn't have to work so hard to keep someone interested. I hope I managed to convince him that even though I'm not the best looking I have other things to offer.

C. FORMATIVE FIRSTS: PRESSURE TO PUT OUT/PERFORM: Because I don't think of myself as being the best looking, I'll have to compensate by being really fun in bed and being willing to experiment and dressing to please. In the past this has meant faking orgasms and pretending to like things that made me uncomfortable.

D. PREVIOUS RELATIONSHIPS: Here we go again. I have to spend the first several months pretending to be fun-loving and adventurous when most of the time, I'd rather order in dinner and watch late-night television or play Boggle. But if I want to wind up married with kids before I'm too old, what choice do I have?

E. CURRENT DATING PATTERNS: What the hell happened? I have no idea if we actually connected or I'm just happy that he seemed to like me so much. I feel like I did a really good job in seeming like the kind of person he'd want. I think I looked good enough and pretended to be sexually daring by referring to a wild phase in college that never really happened (unless reading Judy Blume counts), and I acted like I was super-mellow even though I freak out when there's a single dish in the sink overnight. I also said I could bake cookies, which is true, but not from scratch like I pretended. I guess I can always learn. I hope he likes me. I can worry about whether I like him later!

Did you make it through all five milestones, or do you still have some left to finish? If so, you can finish tomorrow. And don't worry if you didn't analyze each milestone through all the lenses. Pick the lens that has had the biggest effect on the milestone. Take a few deep breaths and decompress.

See you tomorrow.

Day 28

After you finish your breathing exercises, I want you to take a look at what you wrote down yesterday. Now go through each of the milestones again quickly, and write about the positive thoughts and feelings you would need to have in order to approach each milestone healthfully.

This is not to say we will not hear our parents' voices whispering in our heads about how it's time to get married and settle down, or that we will not look in the mirror and see the chubby adolescent we once were instead of the fit and attractive adult we've grown into. But once we recognize that we can control (and subsume) all these negative influences, we have the power to rethink them rationally. So returning to what Olivia wrote yesterday, here's how she wrote about the second and third milestones:

2. Anticipation of the second and third dates when you think there might be something there
3. Sex with a prospective partner for the first time

> A. FAMILY VALUES: I would never want to be in a marriage like my parents had. I'd rather be single for the rest of my life than serve my husband coffee every morning like I'm some friggin' waitress. If this man is anything like my father, I wouldn't want him. If he's the sort of person who is interested in a partnership and not a stultifying conventional relationship, I am definitely excited about getting to know him better!
>
> B. EARLY SOCIALIZATION: INSECURITY/FEAR OF REJECTION: I always had a number of close friends who thought the world of me (it was mutual, of course). If there is some genuine compatibility, this guy will be really happy to have me in his corner. I'm a super listener, a very loyal friend, and extremely insightful to boot. I love meeting people and doing things, and I think we could have a

really good time together, provided he has the energy to keep up!

C. **FORMATIVE FIRSTS: PRESSURE TO PUT OUT/PERFORM**: Once I get past being nervous, I really do love being touched and having sex. If I weren't so worried about how long it takes me to come, in fact, I would have had a lot of sex more often. This time, I'm not going to fake it. I'm going to be confident that the fact that I really enjoy pleasuring someone, and being pleased, is enough to make me a desirable partner.

D. **PREVIOUS RELATIONSHIPS**: I'm not going to make the same mistakes again. I will decide if I like him without getting blindsided by whether or not he likes me! I have a wonderful, meaningful career and a load of great friends and an active social life. And if he can't add to that in a positive way, I will wait for someone who can.

E. **CURRENT DATING PATTERNS**: I'm going to live in the here and now, and I'm going to listen! I'll spend more time thinking about whether he is the kind of person I would want as my friend and lover than worrying whether I'm coming off as too uptight, or too eager or too anything else for that matter. I'm going to be me and let him be him and we'll just see if that leads us down the same path or different ones. Either way, it's okay. I know I have a lot to offer and eventually I will find someone worthy of my endless energy and affection.

Now it's your turn. Like Olivia, feel free to combine milestones, or even the lenses through which I've asked you to see them—the key is to try to overcome the negative associations with powerful affirmative ones.

Then take a few deep breaths and decompress.

You're almost there!

See you tomorrow.

Day 29

Really focus on clearing your thoughts today when you do your breathing exercises.

As always, I saved the best for last: SEX!! How well do you know what you want in bed and out? How aware are you of your erotic turn-ons and emotional needs and how do they factor into your ability to sustain a healthy sex life within a long-term relationship?

Circle the nine statements that most closely resonate with what you want in a sexually intimate relationship.

1. I want my partner to show me how hot he or she finds me without having to say it.

2. I want my partner to ache with desire for me.

3. I want my partner to rip my clothes off and do me on the kitchen counter.

4. I want to writhe with anticipation over a romantic dinner for two.

5. I want my partner to talk dirty to me and make me wait until I'm ready to beg.

6. I want to have crazy knock-down, drag-out sex with my partner until we pass out.

7. I want my partner to seduce me.

8. I want my partner to want to do things with/to me in bed that he or she never did with anyone else before.

9. I want my pulse to race when my partner touches me.

10. I want to get turned on just by the thought of having sex with my partner.

11. I want my partner to be desperate at the thought of us breaking up.

12. I want my partner to be jealous of other men/women.

13. I want my partner to want to spend more time with me.

14. I want my partner to tell me that I'm the best lover he or she ever had.

15. I don't want my partner to have any secrets.

16. I want my partner to say we'll be together forever.

17. I want my partner to say I'm the love of his or her life.

18. I want my partner to send me love letters, buy me little gifts, and leave little love notes on the refrigerator.

19. I want my partner to swear he or she will never love someone else, even if I died.

20. I want my partner to be so content he or she can't even fantasize about another woman or man.

21. I want my partner to make me laugh.

22. I want to have great conversations with my partner and never get bored.

23. I want my partner to stand by me through good times and bad.

24. I want my partner to be trustworthy, loyal, and truthful.

25. I want my partner to know how I'd react to something without having to ask.

26. I want my partner to remember anniversaries, birthdays, and other important occasions.

27. I want my partner to really like my friends and family.

28. I want my partner to be open to change.

29. I want my partner to respect me and be supportive of my decisions.

30. I want my partner to grow old with me.

Look over the nine statements you selected:

FOR EVERY STATEMENT FROM 1–10 that you selected, add 1 point.
FOR EVERY STATEMENT FROM 11–20 that you selected, add 2 points.
FOR EVERY STATEMENT FROM 21–30 that you selected, add 3 points.

What does your score mean?

If you scored under 15, your ideal relationship is defined largely by lust, rather than a deeper emotional connection. Chances are you may not yet be ready to give up the single life.

If you scored between 15 and 24, your ideal relationship would be categorized as one of romantic love or infatuation, one that is the stuff of long-term dreams. You are probably ready and eager to commit.

If you scored more than 24, you are eager to zoom past the hot sex phase right into the attachment phase. You are probably not a sexual thrill-seeker, but someone who prefers to feel safe and secure.

In my experience, not only do all long-lasting, satisfying relationships progress through all three stages—lust, romantic love, and attachment—but those relationships that survive the test of time are able to hold onto aspects from each of the key dimensions. Think about what your answers say about what you want in a relationship, and write about your feelings in your Detox Diary. Take a deep breath. Only one day left!

See you tomorrow.

Day 30

Congratulations! You have completed the detox phase of your program. I know it may have been a long, difficult process at times, and that I asked you to do a lot of thinking and writing. Even though I've structured the program to unfold over thirty days, it's highly possible that there were areas you glossed over or would like to go back to. Maybe you're ready to jump back in the saddle and start dating again. Maybe you need some more time. Do what's right for you. The key to reentering the dating world as a happier, healthier single person is knowing yourself, foibles and all, and realizing that those early experiences don't define you, nor are they fundamentally good or bad. They are simply what has made you who you are. Learning to move beyond the negativity and developing healthy new patterns that incorporate all the constructive, empowering aspects of your past will enable you to embark on more satisfying long-term relationships. Of course, developing lasting emotional attachments and sexual intimacy takes lots of practice and hard work. And this detox program is only the beginning, but hopefully it provides a fresh start that will enable you to truly live your love life to the fullest.

As the final component of your Detox, I want you to reread your Detox Diary and think about all of the positive influences versus the ones that have been toxic to your emotional well-being and that have contributed to your previous negative dating patterns. If you feel that there are areas you'd like to explore further, consider taking some time to peruse or even work through some of the modules in the Couples' Detox that might be relevant regardless of your relationship state: Module 3: Sexual Socialization (page 56), Module 4: Previous Relationships (page 72), and Module 5: Navigating Your Love Map (page 85) will help deepen your detox experience.

See you tomorrow, or whenever you're ready, for the rejuvenation program.

10.

The Singles' Rejuvenation: Dating Inside Out

When talking to couples about the Rejuvenation, I usually begin by introducing the concept of "sensate focus," or touching exercises, as a means of taking baby steps back into the world of sex. As the term suggests, sensate focus underscores the experience of sensations and is used to strengthen the synergy between mind and body. *As it turns out, this approach is even more critical when you are single.* Learning to get centered and being able to develop a keener sense of who and what turns you on is vital not only to searching for dates, but in gauging compatibility and sustaining sexual chemistry and emotional fulfillment over the long haul. So think of the rejuvenation phase of this program as "sensate dating"— attuning your instincts and responses to all the various sensations, and dating sensationally as well. We'll do this through three stages:

Stage One: **Stepping Out**
Stage Two: **Stop, Drop, and Listen**
Stage Three: **Ten First Dates**

But unlike the detox program, which was fairly regimented in how it unfolded day to day, the rejuvenation phase doesn't follow a particular schedule. Rather, think of it as a series of best practices that you should be integrating into your love life and making your own as you get out there and start dating again. The point of the Detox was to provide you with a fresh start, and now it's time to make the most of that start.

STAGE ONE: STEPPING OUT

Tell the truth. Have you fallen back into old habits? Perhaps just a little? You know the ones I'm referring to—the constant checking of email for winks and blinks and maybe drinks. Are you describing yourself as wild and adventurous when your idea of a good time is an old Hepburn/Tracy flick and a warm slice of home-baked apple crisp? Before you do anything else, I want you to examine your behavior over the last few days. In what ways are you repeating old patterns? Have you found yourself slipping back into the familiar comfort of your old standards? If you find out so-and-so has all the qualities you always thought you wanted, but none of the traits you need, are you still pursuing contact? When you are communicating with a prospective date, whether by email, instant message, phone, or in person, are you too busy listening to yourself and measuring how well you are holding up to your projected image of yourself to notice whether you really click with the other person? Are you dating in the moment or in the past?

Conversely, if you haven't dated in a while or have very little experience when it comes to dating, what is it that has prevented you from being out there? Was it a single bad experience, or have you simply just not done it much? If it's the latter, is it lack of opportunity, or a lack of desire on your part? Perhaps it's simply a confidence issue. If so, what clear action-oriented steps can you take to start dating with confidence?

It's a Date!

During the next few days, you are going to seek out, accept, and plan an actual date. No exes. This may take a few days or a week or longer. That honestly doesn't matter. The most important thing is that you only set up a date with someone who meets the criteria you are looking for now and that you only project yourself as you are, not who you believe they want you to be. No more dissembling. And no more posturing. If they ask if you'd like to go to a science fiction movie marathon and you'd rather listen to nails on a chalkboard, say so (though you can be a bit more polite). If what you really want to do is go to an exhibit at the planetarium, suggest it. Be yourself. This will give the other person the courage to be honest, too.

Manage Your Expectations

The idea here is to open your eyes and see new possibilities. That means taking risks. It also means giving someone a chance because there's something about them you like even if, *especially* if, they are different from anyone you've ever dated before. Again, pay attention to your own sense of excitement and what the other person has to say. It's important to approach new dates the way you would any social event, with a sense of fun and excitement. Chances are this will not be the person who fetches your dentures in your declining years. But so the heck what? It's just a first date, got it? Learn to be in the moment, enjoy it for what it is, and see where it all leads without getting burdened by possibility or weighed down by past disappointments or future imperatives.

Enjoy Yourse*lf*

For many of us, the best part of going out somewhere nice is the opportunity to dress up and play grown up. Feeling sexy in your skin is a vital part of dating in the moment. So take some time to prepare. If you can swing it, get something new to wear. If time permits, schedule a haircut or a facial or even a pedicure. This goes for guys as well (well, maybe not the pedicure). Take your time showering and shaving. Revel in feeling sexy and alive and ripe with possibility. Think about all the wonderful things you've seen and done and would like to do that you want to share. Most of all, delight in being in your own head, rather than trying to read someone else's mind to see what they think about you. Test yourself throughout the evening and make sure you are really listening actively and participating honestly. Remember what we learned about rewiring? It's all about practice. So use this as an opportunity to start building healthier dating and relating patterns.

Time to ReORDER

At some point during your date, I want you to excuse yourself and re-group. Then run a quick self-analysis session.

Observe—Are you dating in the moment? Or are you watching yourself from the sidelines?

Recognize—Are you haunted by the memories of things past?

De-couple—Are you approaching things in a new way?

Engage—Are you actively tuning into how this person makes you feel?

Regulate—Are you checking yourself so you don't lapse into old patterns?

Now get back out there. Even if you know this person is simply not right for you, practice makes perfect, or at least it makes better. So take advantage of the fact that you probably won't ever go out with this person again and take a few extra risks. If they ask whether you liked their favorite movie, and you didn't, say so. If they want to know what you'd like for dessert and you are on a diet, say so. If they say something that offends you, tell them you find dirty knock-knock jokes about chicks with big boobs juvenile and unsexy. I'm not saying you should be rude, but go the extra yard and really enjoy the freedom of being you, uncensored.

Swing Low, Sweet Harriet

Before we move onto the next stage, let's take an up close and personal look at Stage One in action. Harriet, a divorced thirty-nine-year-old schoolteacher from Montclair, New Jersey, undertook the Dating Detox with a daunting sense of deliberation. She retraced. She explored. She filled her memory box and then emptied it again, eliminating all the negative associations and experiences and replacing them with fruitful future fantasies. She went into the Rejuvenation thoroughly rejuvenated. She was ready to go. She was hot in her skin. She swept her online dating profiles clean and started out fresh.

Lo and behold she soon lined up a date with a guy who seemed completely different from anyone she'd ever gone out with before (including her crummy ex-husband). When he asked what she wanted to do, instead of agreeing to dinner on Friday night, she suggested trapeze school on Saturday morning. And that is exactly what they did on their date.

It didn't take Harriet long to realize that Vic made her sick. He was gruff, controlling, and downright handsy. And while she'd hoped for someone who was not uptight and pretentious like her ex, she wasn't itching for Tony Soprano, either. She got on the trapeze, and he immediately whistled a catcall from the sidelines, hollering "nice dish, baby," as she swung in her padded bike shorts and tank top for all the world to see. And instead of focusing on what he was focusing on, namely, the size of her derriere from that particular vantage, Harriet screamed out, "Too bad, you'll never get a bite." The upshot was a rousing round of applause and another date from another guy with a better butt, to boot.

STAGE TWO: STOP, DROP, AND LISTEN

So here you are again, home, alone after your first foray back into the fabulous feats of dating. You can practically hear the Coffee Heath Bar Crunch in the freezer calling out delicious obscenities (eat me, lick me) in your direction. Your email is desperately waiting to be clicked open. Your best friend is undoubtedly home from a date, too, itching like poison oak in summer stretch pants to hear all about how bad your night was. Remember that old adage you learned back in kindergarten regarding what to do in case of fire? Then heed the smoke signals and run for cover: Stop, drop, and listen!

Maybe you're proud of how well you did tonight and want to brag to your former college roommate about the fact that you dated in the moment. Maybe you are wildly disappointed because you didn't truly manage your expectations and thought, after all your hard work, wouldn't it be sort of cool and funny, kind of like kismet, if this turned out to be "the one"? Or maybe, and believe me this is the worst of all possible maybes, maybe you are plum unsure and could use a little interpretive guidance from a half-dozen or so of your closest friends.

Whatever it is you usually did after your first dates (including doing your first date), resist the urge. Instead I want you to take a few deep breaths and really think about how your evening (or afternoon or morning trapeze session) went, whether you were genuinely present during the majority of the date and if you'd like to see this person again.

Tell Me about You: What Do YOU Think about ME?
Once, again, I'm going to ask you to circle all those that apply:

1. I wonder whether he or she liked me.

2. Did he or she seem amused or grossed out when I talked about the guy in my office who brings his laptop and rubber stress ball to the bathroom?

3. Holy crap! I should never have ordered that third glass of rum and Diet Coke: Just look at the way my stomach is hanging out over my belt!

4. Please tell me that speck of parsley wasn't there since the appetizer course!

5. Why didn't he or she talk about going on another date? Or was he or she only pretending when he or she said we *should* do this again?

6. Man, my friend [fill in the blank] would think he or she was totally smokin'. OR Man, my friend [fill in the blank] would think he or she was a lame-ass loser! I can't wait to tell [fill in the blank] all about this!

7. If that idiot doesn't email or call me for another date, it means I'll never find anyone in this miserable singles' market.

8. I can't believe [fill in the blank] would set me up with someone who dresses like that! Ugh.

9. Do I call him/her back in two days or three days? Will two days seem desperate? Will he or she be married to someone else in three days?

Of course, insecurity is inevitable. But it's important for you learn to understand and manage those feelings that will wind up depleting your confidence and self-esteem. This is why it is so critical that you take some time to understand where these feelings are coming from before you resort to old behaviors or add external noise (like what your former roommate or ex would think if he or she met so-and-so). Instead, I want you to transpose your focus to what *you* thought of your date, without undue emphasis on what you think *he or she* thought about *you*. Got it?

Chemistry 101. Time for a Pop Quiz

1. So tell me, did you like him or her? No, no. I didn't ask whether you thought he or she liked you. I said did *you* like him or her?

2. Did you find yourself suppressing the desire to roll your eyes more than once?

3. Did you feel your pulse jump when you made eye contact?

4. Did your mouth go dry?

5. Would you want to know what your date would think about a recent article you read on your favorite news site?

6. Do you assume you would find his or her friends more engaging or offensive?

7. By the end of the date, could you already predict nearly everything he or she had to say? Or did you find yourself delightfully surprised at the unusual way his or her mind worked?

8. Did you get a strange warm gooey feeling that you'd somehow known this person all your life?

9. Does the thought of having sex with him or her induce excitement, disgust, or sleep?

10. Do you want to see this person again? I didn't ask whether you wanted to spend the rest of your life with him or her, or whether you heard wedding bells, just whether you felt enough to want to go out *one more time*.

I don't want to insult your intelligence by telling you what you already know. But before you spend one moment laboring and fretting over what this person thought about you, I want you to determine whether or not you and your date clicked, from your own perspective. Would *you* want to know this person better? What if he or she were a married colleague at work? Would you want to chat with this person over coffee? Now, I want you to think about the four dimensions of compatibility we discussed. Did this person have the particular qualities that matter to you? Not to your friends or your family or the world at large, but *to you*?

Please don't get me wrong here. I'm not saying that it's either love at first sight or call it quits at the get-go. What I am saying is that there are perfectly good reasons why most of those dates *you didn't like* didn't call for a second date. And even if you were too wrapped up in wanting them to like you to notice, there was a lack of something going on. So this time, I want you to assess whether there was sufficient chemistry to warrant another date before you go hemming and hawing and triple-checking your answering machine and composing and deleting emails by the dozens. If there was something worth pursuing, that's great. That's also not a reason to stop dating other people. It may just mean you are more comfortable and happy with who you are and simply enjoying yourself.

If, on the other hand, you felt like there was an absolute disconnect, consider this done. Move on. I don't care if this person is the end-all and be-all of Hollywood romance personified and exactly the kind of guy or gal your mother always hoped you'd bring home to Thanksgiving dinner. I don't care if your friends would swoon with jealousy. You need to learn how to trust your instincts this go around. Don't fall into the trap of worrying about whether they follow up. Don't become obsessed with going out with them because they had the good sense not to like you and must, therefore, be a catch. Move on!

Hurry Up and Wait

What next? Say you had a reasonably good time on your date. Do you call? If so, when? Do you play it cool or turn up the heat?

I should say from the outset that I am no advocate of *The Rules*. It is my feeling that if you had a nice time on the date and would like to see the person again, you should follow up sometime over the next day or two to say so. It shows a level of confidence that anyone with half a brain will find appealing. If, for whatever reason, your date doesn't share your enthusiasm, you need to realize it has nothing to do with you. I know: Easier said than done. But honestly, who knows what (or who) else they have on their plate? You just met them. Just let it go. And move on. Dating should be fun. If it's not, it's time to go back and do a little reORDERing before you dive back in again.

STAGE THREE: TEN FIRST DATES

Earlier, I told you I was going to ask you to go out on a single date with a set of fresh eyes.

I'm sorry to report that I sort of fibbed.

I'd like you to go on *ten* first dates—and I mean that literally: ten first dates without the expectation of a second one. Doing this will relieve the pressure and allow you to widen your scope and date people you might not have previously considered. And, as it turns out, in picking ten (as opposed to five or seventeen) I'm using the science of the numbers.

Let me explain.

Cognitive science all-stars Peter Todd, Ph.D., at Indiana University in Bloomington, and Geoffrey Miller, Ph.D., at the University of New Mexico, used advanced computer simulations to examine the thorny field of "mate-choice" to determine the best system to find lasting love. They wrote about their findings in a chapter of an anthology entitled *Simple Heuristics That Make Us Smart*. (Heuristics is basically a fancy term for problem solving, or the art of picking a few shorthand rules to help us make complex decisions, and what's more complex than solving the problem of how to date more efficiently and effectively?)

Todd and Miller began (but did not end) their theoretical pursuit of the ideal search process by first applying a well-known system of hypothetical choice making, the "secretary problem," to dating. The "secretary problem" describes a situation in which *one must pick the very best secretary* from a group of applicants who appear in random order, drawn from a pool whose quality is not known. Once rejected, applicants cannot be recalled.

While the secretary problem is theoretical, it's relevant to dating in that "it directly addresses what to do about the uncertainty that the next prospect one encounters might be far superior to the best seen so far." Sound familiar? Who hasn't rejected a perfect candidate because of the fantasy that the person around the corner will be better? There's more. According to Todd and Miller, "It can be shown that the solution to the secretary problem demands sampling a certain proportion of the applicants, remembering the best of them, and then picking the next applicant who is even better." In other words we can come up with a perfect number of dates for you.

So how many "applicants" does one have to "sample" in order to make a smart, effective decision? In the secretary problem, the ideal percentage for sampling, based on an overall pool of one hundred applicants, is 37 percent. That means it would make sense to initially sample thirty-seven of them, remember the best of the best, and then pick the next candidate who meets or exceeds that best candidate.

Now in the real world of dating the pool of potential candidates is much bigger than one hundred people, and for many of us it would be too tiring to go out and date thirty-seven people, especially if we then had to keep dating to find someone who was better than the best candidate. You might also be saying, *"Please* I've already dated my thirty-seven guys or gals, I don't need to sample any more candidates. I'm sampled to death!"

Rest assured: While I am not going to ask you to go out and date thirty-seven people, I am going to ask you to date a certain set number of people with a fresh set of eyes, and not to focus on any of those people as potentially being "the one." Rather, view them as a research project of sorts in which you have no intention of ever seeing them again.

Why do I want you to do this? Because the detox program should leave you with a new attitude, and I want you to use that attitude to set your "aspiration level"—based on a realistic view of who's available and who you can attract (with the highest possible "mate value," as Todd and Miller would put it)—without wasting your time by dating ad nauseam.

So how many dates do we need to go on to set a realistic aspiration level and find lasting love? Isn't the 37 percent number suggested by the "secretary system" too unrealistic and daunting? Todd and Miller certainly thought so, and recognized that in the real world of dating, the "secretary problem" approach doesn't quite cut it.

Going back to their advanced computer simulations, Miller and Todd raised the number of potential candidates from one hundred to one thousand and proved, to the relief of all us out there dating, that a little bit of searching does indeed goes a long way. According to their research, in a group of one thousand, "Only 3 percent of the potential mates need to be checked to set the aspiration level, and for a mate in the top 25 percent, only 1 to 2 percent of the potential mates need to be checked. . . . So despite the tenfold increase in population size, the number of individuals to check increases only slightly."

What does all this heuristic-driven scientific research yield, in terms of our dating lives? That you have to go on roughly ten first dates. If after ten dates there's someone you want to go back to and he or she is available, then go for it. But give yourself those ten first dates.

So get out there with a fresh set of eyes and set your aspiration level. And remember that part of the fun of going on ten first dates is there's no pressure to have a second date, so take some risks and let yourself be surprised.

When Carrie Met Sally

Carrie came to see me the day after she turned thirty-five. A successful entrepreneur, she'd pocketed a handsome sum of money in the boom of the dot-com era. Thus, she was fortunate to have the flexibility to work as an independent business consultant. Having spent the majority of her twenties and early thirties working more than one hundred hours a week, however, she'd never had a whole lot of time to pursue relationships. She'd had plenty of flings and a few long-term liaisons, but they'd always been built for convenience rather than passion. At age thirty-five, Carrie assessed the situation and mapped out a plan. Either she would find a partner within one year or she would have a child on her own.

Wanting to make her search as efficient and productive as possible, Carrie came in and told me her drop-dead date for finding a life partner. I tried not to laugh (or cry). When I asked her what kind of people she'd found herself attracted to in the past, she drew a complete blank and then said simply, "nobody clingy." Yikes.

Like a trooper, she went through the Detox and did her exercises, although I never got the sense she was doing it in earnest. It was simply something she felt compelled to do in order to get on with the business of life. In reviewing her history, I learned Carrie was an only child who'd grown up in Manhattan and attended a prestigious private school. Her parents had divorced when she was in grade school. Her mother never expressed any interest in dating. Instead she threw herself into her career, rising to the level of chief of operations for a medium-sized marketing firm. When Carrie came to her with questions about sex, her mother gave her volumes of illustrated books on the subject and told her to speak with her nanny, who unfortunately mainly spoke French.

Carrie dutifully came up with a list of early sexual forays that included a smattering of positive erotic memories. As far as actual love was concerned, however, she didn't remember feeling that emotionally connected to any of her partners, from adolescence through adulthood. By the time the Detox was over, she was eager to get the ball rolling and go about finding herself a mate—that is, someone who was more or less her mirror image.

After going out on about ten dates, she went back and chose her favorite of the lot and asked him out again. They went out for several months and mutually decided it was time to make it official. A wedding was put into the works. When she came in and thanked me for helping her achieve her objective, I felt my heart drop. There was no change in Carrie. No sign of warmth or giddy excitement. No tenderness. But she was now engaged and planning to get married.

Ordinarily, I make it a point of not questioning people about their ultimate choices. If they ask me for help, I am there to help foster their emotional and sexual development. But otherwise, I try to resist the urge to interfere. But this time, I made an exception. I felt like my approach had failed her, and that at the very least I owed her a final session to talk things out. Being busy, Carrie said she appreciated the offer, but declined.

A few weeks later, I received a voicemail marked "urgent." Carrie said she needed to meet with me at once. In my office, she explained that when she went in for a fitting at the bridal salon, she had been introduced to the proprietor, Sally, a striking woman in her early forties who had, ironically enough, made a career of designing bridal gowns although she herself had never been married. While she pinned and fitted and fussed with Carrie's bows and netting, the two women talked and laughed for hours. Later that evening, she called her fiancé and told him she was having some concerns. Thinking it was just a case of wedding jitters, he didn't take Carrie's misgivings seriously and agreed to discuss it when he returned from a business conference in Geneva. But Carrie was extremely serious about her doubts.

Feeling a bit frazzled, she asked Sally to join her for dinner. Carrie and Sally went to a charming French bistro. The conversation was witty and engaging. She felt comfortable yet giddy. Her senses seemed to come alive. When she went into the bathroom to powder her nose, she looked at her glowing complexion in the mirror and gasped. There was no doubt about it: She was attracted to Sally.

As Carrie told me about Sally, her face grew flushed, and she smiled like I'd never seen her before. And I knew, from her joyous expression, that the feelings had been very much reciprocated. She was truly falling in love for the first time ever.

So what is my point in telling you this? The goal of this program is not to find a spouse for the sake of being married. The goal is to get rid of your prefabricated pictures and checklists and learn to trust your own instincts. And then to follow them wherever they lead you, even if it's someplace you never dreamed you'd go.

I often tell people that dating and maintaining relationships—finding and sustaining love—is like acquiring a piece of art: We should wait to be struck and captivated by someone we want to take home and frame. But all too often we do the opposite: We walk around with our "frames," desperately trying to fit others into them. Not only do we get stuck on a fixed idea of whom we should be with, but we carry those frames with us into our intimate relationships, where they shape our expectations and, ultimately, our disappointments. Our frames are narrow and confining, offering only a tiny window into the world through which we are constantly "looking" rather than truly "seeing." Worse, our frames also become shields, blocking others from getting through.

I sincerely hope that this process of dating detoxification and rejuvenation has provided you with the inspiration and fortification to question and dismantle your frames: to not only let yourself see people for who they are, but to know yourself and truly be seen for who you are.

You only have one love life, so live it to the fullest!

If you have questions or comments, visit www.IanKerner.com, where you will find additional content, a community, and a growing directory of resources to supplement your journey.

ACKNOWLEDGMENTS

First and foremost, I would like to thank all the men and women who participated in this program in its various stages of evolution and contributed to its refinement. Thank you for letting me work on your love lives from the inside out.

Thank you to everyone at Collins for treating me so well. Your enthusiasm, support, intelligence, and warmth are graciously appreciated.

To my editor, Cassie Jones, what a journey it's been! I can't tell you how glad it makes me to know that it's always you on the other side of the phone.

To my friend and agent, Richard Abate, thank you for always being the first to act on my behalf and always knowing the next right move.

To Peter Hyman and Sue Rosenstock, thank you for all of your editorial contributions and finesse.

To my wife, Lisa, thank you for putting up with me and always being my light at the end of the tunnel.

INDEX

Johns Hopkins University, 22
Johnson, Virginia, 121
journaling, 29–30. *See also* writing
  on attractiveness misconceptions,
    172–74
  breathing thoughts/emotions,
    connections between, 30, 31,
    142–43
  on dating, 161–64, 166–67
  helps/hurts, 163–64
  on masturbation, 40–41
  past influences/influencers, 171–72
  pros/cons of childhood/adolescence,
    153–54
  sex, what is wanted from, 210–12
  on virginity, 78–79
  on worst breakups, 199–200

kissing, 74–75, 124

Lamm, Steven, *The Hardness Factor*,
  44
l-arginine, 49
lesbian, 60
letting go, 200–201
libido reduction, 49–50
light kissing, 74–75
lights off sex, 132–34
limits, testing, 96–98
looks, 155
love map
  definition of, 22–23
  navigating, 85–100
lust, 212

male brain, 128
massage, 70. *See also* touching
  caressing v., 124
Masters, William, 121
masturbation, 33, 123
  fantasies during, 41
  home environment and, 69–70
  journaling on, 40–41
mate. *See also* partner
  dimensions for assessing, 192, 221
  friend v., 195–96, 197
  ideal, 155–57, 192–202, 226
  income bracket criteria for, 162

  long-term, readiness for, 203–5
  prospective, 192–202, 223–24
media imagery, 23, 85, 173
meeting people, 186–87
memories
  arousal, 84
  erotic, 86–91, 93
memory box, 40
menopause, 59
ME time. *See* module ending
milestones in dating, 206–7, 209
Miller, Geoffrey, *Simple Heuristics That
  Make us Smart*, 222–24
*The Mind and the Brain: Neuroplasticity and
  the Power of Mental Force* (Schwartz/
  Begley), 16–17
mindfulness, art of, 16–17
mind stimulation, 129
minerals, arousal and, 49
misconceptions, attractiveness, 172–74
"Modern Love" (Yoder), 12
module duration, 28
module ending (ME time), 42, 43, 55, 84
  diary review, 115–16
  fantasy centered, 99–100
  for singles, 157–58, 191
mom, unsexy, 31
Money, John, 22

National Institute of Mental Health, 122
navigating love map, 85–100
negative home environment, 68, 77
neurochemistry, 10–13, 137
  summary of, 10–11
neuroplasticity, 14–15, 16–17
neurotransmitters. *See* dopamine
newness, 11, 110, 133
New Scientist, 122
nitric oxide, 45
norepinephrine, 11
nurturing, stimulation v., 126

observation stage, 19, 61, 179, 217
obsessive compulsive dating, 15–16,
  161–64
obsessive compulsive disorder (OCD), 15,
  16–17
obstacles, sexual satisfaction, 113–15

OCD. *See* obsessive compulsive disorder
omega-3s, 49
oral sex, 75–77, 93
organizations, counseling, 106
orgasm, 112. *See also* sexual satisfaction
  fake, 113–15, 123, 130–32
  female, 127
  heart attacks and, 44
outlook. *See* attitude
overdating, 186
oxytocin, 117, 122
  hugging/gender and, 122–23

parents, 31, 35, 36, 150–51, 173, 208
participation, partner, 7–8
partner. *See also* mate
  activities with, 108–9
  attractiveness of, 110–12
  attributes of, listing positive/negative,
    110–11
  behavior of, 54–55
  checking in with, 55
  communication with, 118–21, 132
  not participating in detox, 7–8
  potential, 146, 192–202
  reviewing diary with, 118–21
  same-sex, case studies involving, 17–20,
    60–62, 224–26
  sexual chemistry with/desire for, 107–8
  sexual experiences reviewed by, early, 133
past
  ghosts of, 199–200
  journaling on, 171–72
permissive home environment, 67–68
personality, 192, 193, 196
PET. *See* positron emission tomography
photo collecting, 58, 172
physical attractiveness, 192, 193, 194, 195,
    221. *See also* sexual chemistry
physical intimacy, non-sexual, 106–7
physical wellness, 47, 51–52
planning, date, 215–16
plateau, 112
Plato, 23
playing house, 18
poles, four fantasy, 130–32
positive-negative interaction ratio, 120–21
positron emission tomography (PET), 128

predominantly nurturing environment, 67
premise, 3
previous relationships, 72–84
profile, dating, 165
prospective dates, meeting, 186–87
prospective mate, 192–202, 223–24
pycnogenol, 49

qualities
  dimensions of, 192, 221
  expanding horizons for sought out,
    195–97, 202
  friend v. mate, 195–96
  ideal mate, 192–202
  instincts about, 226
  must-have, 200
questionnaire. *See also* detox diagnostic;
    journaling
  affection, 59–60
  current relationship, 102–4
  dating, 143–49, 166–69, 183–84
  desire for partner, 107–8
  erotic memory, 89–91
  fantasy, 86, 93–95, 96–97
  fantasy comfort zone, 96–97
  formative firsts, 83–84
  gender stereotype, 63–66, 175–77
  influences/influencers, 171–72
  relationship dreams, 80–82
  relationship readiness, long-term, 203–5
  sexual chemistry, 107–8, 220–21
  toxicity, 143–49

raking, 124
rapid ejaculation, 129
Ratey, John J., *A User's Guide to the Brain,*
    14, 15
ratio, positive-negative interaction, 120–21
readiness
  commitment, 212
  dating, 203–13
  for long-term relationship, 203–5
recognition stage, 19, 61, 120, 180, 217
regulating stage, reORDERing process,
    20, 61, 62, 120, 181, 217
rejuvenation
  couples', 117–34
  pace of, 118